People

GONE
TOO
SOON

CONTENTS

GONE TOO SOON

An astonishing fact: When Elvis Presley died in 1977, PEOPLE did not put him on the cover. Instead, the magazine addressed the King's untimely passing with one picture, one paragraph and 171 words, in Star Tracks—right above an item about a new Dorothy Hamill ice-skating doll.

Looking back, it seems like a jaw-dropping decision. But we, the editors, meant no disrespect: The magazine was new and still struggling every week to define what it was and learn what readers wanted. Quite simply, we thought that, for a magazine that thrived on the headlong energy of celebrity and popular culture, death was too morbid a subject for the cover. Readers, we feared, would recoil.

We were, of course, unquestionably, stupendously wrong. Readers made that clear in December 1980, when John Lennon was murdered.

By then we had realized that when someone famous died, the magazine's audience wanted to connect to the story, immediately: They wanted to know what had happened, and to recall moments in a life they'd followed; many wanted a keepsake. The John Lennon issue became, at the time, the best-selling issue PEOPLE had ever published.

Since then, PEOPLE has made a point of covering the passing of famous people, from entertainers like John Belushi and Kurt Cobain to such cultural icons as John F. Kennedy Jr. and Christa McAuliffe to, of course, Princess Diana. The saddest stories are, perhaps, those where the person died young, often suddenly, often at the height of a promising career. This book looks back at those stories, starting with the celebrities who appeared on PEOPLE's covers, from 1974 until the present.

John Lennon
1940-1980
A TRIBUTE

People weekly

DECEMBER 22, 1980 ▪ 95¢

*The murder of an
ex-Beatle shocked the world*

JOHN
LENNON

1940–1980

John Lennon took risks, in music and life. That sense of adventure helped make the Beatles the biggest pop group of all time and his ongoing personal story a headline writer's dream. In 1975 he did it again, something truly revolutionary: Lennon walked away from stardom in an attempt to lead a normal life. He handed his business interests over to his wife, Yoko Ono, and, in their rambling home in New York City's Dakota apartments, became a full-time Mr. Mom to his son Sean. He discovered he loved it. "Sean is my biggest pride, you see," he said. "And you're talking to a guy who was not interested in children at all before—they were just sort of things that were around, you know?" He also loved the pace, living a comparatively normal life in a comparatively normal neighborhood. "I can go out right now and go into a restaurant," he told a BBC interviewer on Dec. 6, 1980. "People will come up and ask for autographs, but they don't bug you."

Two days later, as he entered the Dakota on the night of Dec. 8, Lennon, 40, was shot and killed by Mark David Chapman. Holding a copy of *The Catcher in the Rye*,

Twist and shout: John, Paul, George and Ringo during the early, classic mop-top era.

Chapman waited calmly for police. A troubled young man who had drifted through a series of low-paying jobs and had twice attempted suicide, Chapman later told *The New York Times* that the book would explain his motives. At his arraignment he originally pleaded not guilty by reason of insanity but later decided to plead guilty to second-degree murder. He was sentenced to 20 years to life; now residing in New York's Attica Correctional Facility, he has been denied parole four times.

On the afternoon of the murder, Chapman, waiting outside the Dakota, saw Lennon leaving and asked him to autograph a copy of the ex-Beatle's *Double Fantasy* album. Lennon obliged. At that point Chapman, who told police he battled "the Devil" in himself, had second thoughts. "My big part won, and I wanted to go back to my hotel, but I couldn't," he said later. "I waited until he came back."

Lennon and Yoko returned around 10:50 p.m. As they entered the building, Chapman fired several shots, hitting Lennon four times.

To promote peace, John and Yoko stayed in bed for a week in 1969 and gave interviews to reporters.

Thousands gathered in New York City's Central Park, near the Dakota, to mourn Lennon in the days following his murder.

The party never stopped until the night it stopped forever

JOHN BELUSHI

1949–1982

For comedian John Belushi, it was a night like any other: Frantic and drug-fueled, the former *Saturday Night Live* star first stopped, around 9 p.m., at On the Rox, a private club known for spontaneous entertainment provided by visiting stars. Belushi was introduced to singer Johnny Rivers and hung out with actors Robert De Niro and Harry Dean Stanton, television writer Nelson Lyon, and Cathy Smith, a known drug dealer. Later, according to Lyon's court testimony, Belushi returned to his bungalow at the Chateau Marmont and was visited briefly by comedian Robin Williams. At some point after Williams left, Smith injected Belushi with a "speedball," a combination of heroin and cocaine. The next day he was found dead from an overdose.

All who knew him were saddened; few who knew him well were completely surprised. As former *Saturday Night Live* writer Michael O'Donoghue had chillingly observed years before, "The same violent urge that makes John great will also ultimately destroy him. He's one of those hysterical personalities that will never be complete. I look for him to end up floating dead after the party." Belushi— who, an associate noted, ingested everything from "ethyl chloride to Quaaludes"—was not unaware of the risks his lifestyle posed.

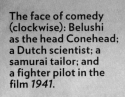

The face of comedy (clockwise): Belushi as the head Conehead; a Dutch scientist; a samurai tailor; and a fighter pilot in the film *1941*.

Belushi "seemed to represent everyone's rebelliousness," said a Second City friend. "He was everyone's free spirit." Pal Dan Aykroyd (left, in leather) and brother Jim Belushi (bearded) helped carry the comedian's casket.

Once, clowning around with *National Lampoon* cofounder Doug Kenney, Belushi had once done an impromptu impression of Elvis Presley in his death throes. Kenney told him it wasn't funny. "But," Belushi replied, "that's the way we're all going to die, Dougie."

Belushi's philosophy was simple and direct: He believed in entertainment, exuberance and anarchy. "What rock and roll was supposed to be about was getting loose, enjoying it, going a little crazy and not caring how you act or dress," he once said. "Now rock and roll is at a standstill, I think—and comedy is taking its place as something exciting."

As a wild man, Belushi, the son of Albanian immigrants who settled in Wheaton, Ill., had been, curiously, something of late bloomer. "Everyone said he was loud and raucous," recalled a childhood neighbor, "but it was always 'Yes, sir' and 'No, sir' with me." He did like attention, and was a star linebacker on his high school football team and elected homecoming king his senior year. At Illinois's College of DuPage, Belushi began doing comedy routines. When Jayce Sloane, an associate producer from Second City, the famous Chicago comedy troupe, called to try to book the group on campus, a DuPage official told her, "We don't need Second City. We've got a student who goes to see your shows and comes back and does it for us." Belushi later auditioned for Second City—and, Sloan recalled, "blew everyone away."

After honing his craft there, he was hired to appear in *National Lampoon's Lemmings* off-Broadway. Many of its stars later joined the original cast of *Saturday Night Live*. "He walked into my office and started to abuse me," *SNL* producer Lorne Michaels recalled. "He said, 'I can't stand television,' and that was just the kind of abuse I wanted to hear." His performances—as a killer bee, a samurai tailor, Joe Cocker or the "no Coke, Pepsi!" diner owner—were an instant hit with audiences. "[Chevy] Chase was the first star of the show," said NBC exec Dick Ebersol, "but Belushi was the first to become the audience's friend. There was a huge bond." It only grew stronger when Belushi, as proto-frat-boy Bluto Blutarski, an id in a toga, helped make the movie *Animal House* a huge hit.

Belushi is buried on Martha's Vineyard in Massachusetts. His headstone reads, "I may be gone, but rock and roll lives on."

An actress who became royalty, she was, said one friend, "a princess from the moment she was born"

PRINCESS GRACE

1929–1982

Evading police, she raced her blue convertible through the tight curves above Monaco; Cary Grant sat in the passenger seat, looking queasy. Finally, she parked the car at a turnoff and produced a cold-chicken picnic lunch. "A leg or a breast?" she asked naughtily. "You make the choice," he replied, with a faint smile.

That sort of moment, in the film *To Catch a Thief,* captured Grace Kelly's immense appeal: an elegant, patrician glamour wrapped around a sly sensuality. Her first role, as Gary Cooper's wife in 1952's *High Noon,* made her a star; the next five years produced memorable movies—including *Rear Window, Dial M for Murder* and *The Country Girl,* for which she won an Oscar—and a list of leading men that read like a fantasy Hollywood stag party: Grant, James Stewart, Clark Gable, Bing Crosby, Frank Sinatra. Then, after only 11 films and at the height of her career, Kelly walked away.

Actually, she was swept away. While filming *Thief* she had met Monaco's Prince Rainier III; they wed, with all the pomp and circumstance a glitzy principality could muster, in 1956. (However, she did warn him, later, that the Kellys of Philadelphia, of proud Irish-Catholic descent, were "not impressed by royalty. We're impressed by the man. Marriage is not a game of musical chairs

"I certainly don't think of my life as a fairy tale. I think of myself as a modern, contemporary woman"

Rainier (with daughter Caroline) wept at the funeral.

with us. We play for keeps.") She moved into Rainier's 180-room pink palace, had three children and, through public appearances and charity work, conferred modernity and glamour upon a 467-acre ministate and gambling mecca that had once been famously described, by Somerset Maugham, as "a sunny place for shady people."

Twenty-seven years after filming *To Catch a Thief,* Princess Grace was driving on the same hillside roads when—doctors determined later—she suffered a small stroke and failed to negotiate a steep turn. The car tumbled 120 feet into a garden and burst into flames. Grace's daughter Stephanie, then 17, survived with a cracked vertebra; rushed to a hospital, Grace died the next day from a brain hemorrhage.

Rainier, who seldom let the world see his emotions, wept openly at her funeral. Said a friend: "He is an old man today."

A pioneering anchorwoman lived for the camera and paid a price in her private life

JESSICA SAVITCH

1947–1983

"She was, more than anyone I have ever met, somebody who lived to be on TV."

"From the beginning, from college on, she never had a personal life."

"It was as if she had no other existence outside of when the red light was on."

That was how friends and colleagues described Jessica Savitch: a driven, talented reporter whose own life could be as dramatic as the stories she covered. Her father, a clothing merchant, closely followed the news, so "to win his approval," as she later put it, she did too. Hooked on dreams of a broadcasting career, she became the first anchorwoman in the South and went national, covering the Senate for NBC, in 1977.

On-camera, said one producer, "she felt she had to live out the mythology of TV and be all-wise, all-knowing, as her audiences wanted her to be." Off-camera, "she was none of what people thought she was," said Barbara King, who worked on Savitch's 1982 autobiography, *Anchorwoman.* In the three years before her death, Savitch had endured divorce, a miscarriage and the suicide of her second husband. An on-air segment in which she slurred words and ad-libbed awkwardly fed rumors, rife in the NBC offices, that she was using drugs. But "cocaine was not her problem," said producer and former boyfriend Ron Kershaw. "Ambition was her problem. And that's much worse than any drug."

In the end the dramas of her life played no role in her death. After a quick dinner at a country restaurant, Savitch, 36, and a new beau, Martin Fischbein, driving at night in bad weather, took a wrong turn on a dirt road. Their car flipped upside down into a canal; neither of them survived.

The death of a vibrant young singer—and its surprising cause—shock the culture

KAREN CARPENTER

1950–1983

She did needlepoint, collected Mickey Mouse memorabilia and seldom drank anything harder than iced tea. Her death stunned the country, and not only because of her youth and squeaky-clean image: When Karen Carpenter, half of the 80-million-record-selling brother-sister duo the Carpenters, died of heart failure at 32 in 1983, it was the first time many Americans had ever heard of what, until then, had been a little-understood disease as mysterious as it was potentially deadly: anorexia nervosa.

Despite immense success—the Carpenters' hits "Close to You" and "We've Only Just Begun" were ubiquitous in the '70s—Karen was unhappy with what a friend called her "pear-shaped" figure and tried hard to please her parents and her brother Richard, whom she worshipped. Publicly, she was, like the duo's sweetly optimistic music, always upbeat; a "magical person," in the words of composer Burt Bacharach. But as a doctor at UCLA's Eating Disorders Clinic noted at the time, "It's common for [anorexics] to be sweet. . . . Many keep their emotions inside. They take care of other people, but they don't take care of themselves."

At one point, Carpenter (in 1981) weighed as little as 85 lbs.

Still rocking long after his teen-idol heyday, the singer dies in a plane crash at 45

RICKY NELSON

1940–1985

As Ricky Nelson told the story, it all started the day a high school girlfriend swooned when Elvis came on the radio. "To impress her, I said, 'I'm going to make a record,'" he recalled. Granted, it helped that Nelson already starred, along with his parents, Ozzie and Harriet, and big brother David, in the classic sitcom *The Adventures of Ozzie and Harriet*. Ricky, 16, rounded up some musicians and recorded a cover of the Fats Domino song "I'm Walkin'," and Ozzie decided to include the song on-air. "Nobody realized the power of television," said Ricky. "Within a week, we sold a million records." The process was repeated for songs like "Travelin' Man" and "Hello Mary Lou"; by 21, Nelson had sold close to 35 million records. When he became a LIFE cover boy in 1958, the magazine coined a new term to describe him: Teen Idol.

Nelson's career was eclipsed by the British invasion, and he spent the next decades trying to regain firm footing. His marriage to Kristin Harmon faltered after 14 years and four children. In later years he had a surprise hit with "Garden Party," a wry look at fans who reject a musician's attempts to change. In 1985, at 45, he was still playing clubs and state fairs, as many as 200 nights a year.

That December, on a flight between Alabama and Texas, a faulty heater caused a fire aboard the band's 41-year-old DC-3. The pilot and copilot escaped after making an emergency landing in a pasture, but the flames killed everyone else on board.

Ricky Nelson was a rarity: a teen idol who left a respected musical legacy. He was, as rock critic David Hinckley put it, "the deceptively clean-cut kid" who helped "smuggle rock and roll into America's living rooms."

GONE TOO SOON **23**

The death of a schoolteacher made the shuttle disaster not just powerful but personal

CHRISTA McAULIFFE

1948–1986

Space travel had come to seem so routine that none of the three major TV networks carried the liftoff live. And after nine trips into orbit, the shuttle *Challenger* in particular was deemed particularly safe.

Seventy-three seconds after launch on Jan. 28, 1986, everything changed. First came the explosion, then the sight of hundreds of spectators staring at the sky, wondering if the great flash was merely the routine separation of the first stage. Slowly, agonizingly, faces crumbled and shock settled in.

NASA later determined that a flawed seal had caused *Challenger* to disintegrate, killing astronauts Francis Scobee, Michael Smith, Judith Resnik, Ronald McNair, Ellison Onizuka, Gregory Jarvis and Christa McAuliffe, a New Hampshire teacher who was to become the first United States civilian in space. Too modest to call herself an astronaut—she opted for the self-deprecating "space participant"—McAuliffe, 37, a wife and mother of two, had charmed the public with her enthusiasm and lack of pretense. She was your next-door neighbor, just back from the local market and now on her way into orbit.

McAuliffe had wanted, above all, to teach a lasting lesson about courage and hope. She did.

*Puppy-dog charm
and, in the end, a
heartbreaking habit*

ANDY GIBB

1958–1988

Australian Andy Gibb had just moved to America when his first single, "I Just Want to Be Your Everything," hit No. 1 on U.S. pop charts in 1977. His second single, "(Love is) Thicker than Water," did the same. Ditto his third, "Shadow Dancing." No solo performer had ever done that. It was a breathtaking start: Andy Gibb was 19.

That level of cyclonic celebrity would have been difficult for anyone to handle; for Gibb, baby brother of Barry, Robin and Maurice Gibb of the monster group the Bee Gees, it was impossible. "Superstars usually have a tough hide from having doors slammed in their face and hustling," said a former president of Andy's record label. "Andy never built up those layers because he never had to. Andy grew older, but he never grew up. He was frozen in time at about 17." Performing, he radiated boyish charm; offstage, he was haunted by self-doubt. Said his former agent: "Sometimes I'd say, 'Andy, look in the mirror. You've got everything—good looks, talent. Women love you.' Men liked him too. But when he looked in the mirror, you always had the feeling he didn't see anything."

Gibb filled the emptiness with cocaine, which led to a numbing litany of Troubled Andy stories. He was hired to cohost the dance show *Solid Gold* and appear in the musicals *Pirates of Penzance* and *Joseph and the Amazing Technicolor Dreamcoat*—then fired from each for not showing up. "We'd lose him over long weekends," recalled *Dreamcoat* producer Zev Bufman. "He'd come back Tuesday, and he'd look beat. He was like a little puppy—so ashamed when he did something wrong." At 23, Gibb fell madly in love with, then split from, Victoria Principal, 31. "I just fell apart," he said later. "I started to do cocaine around the clock—about $1,000 a day.... I really think the major reason I fell from stardom was my affair with Victoria." She saw it differently. "I did everything I could," Principal said. "But then I told him he would have to choose between me and his problem."

Gibb finally committed himself to rehab and, by 1988, was living at his brother Robin's Oxfordshire estate and planning a comeback. In March he checked into a hospital, complaining of stomach pains; three days later he died of what doctors determined was an "inflammation of the heart." Although enlargement of the heart is a common side effect of long-term cocaine use, the hospital said a virus might have been the cause.

In Australia, at 19, Gibb had married an 18-year-old receptionist, Kim Reeder, who gave birth to a daughter, Peta, before the marriage fell apart. Although Andy never saw either of them again after 1980, he phoned regularly. Why? "I think," Kim said after hearing of his death, "we were the only touch with reality he ever had."

A crazed fan murders a beautiful young actress—and sends shockwaves through Hollywood

REBECCA SCHAEFFER

1967–1989

She was a beautiful young actress who, at 21, had costarred in a CBS sitcom, *My Sister Sam*, and was beginning to land movie roles. He was nondescript, a guy in a yellow polo shirt who had been seen wandering her L.A. neighborhood, holding out a publicity photo and asking strangers if they knew where Rebecca Schaeffer lived. "I just looked at him and said, 'What?'" recalled a woman who encountered him outside a market. "He looked weird." Another local bumped into him twice. "It was strange seeing him twice," she said. "You think about it for a second and then go your own way. That's what you do in L.A."

Later he was seen getting out of a cab outside Schaeffer's apartment building. Shortly thereafter, neighbors heard a shot and two screams. "It was bloodcurdling," said Richard Goldman, who lived across the street. Another neighbor saw Schaeffer's body lying in her doorway. "Her eyes were open and glazed over," he said. "I took her pulse, and there was no beat." She had been shot once, in the chest. The man in the yellow shirt was seen jogging down the block.

Within days police arrested Robert John Bardo, 19, a troubled fan. A friend of his said Bardo had become obsessed with Schaeffer, written her a love letter and threatened to hurt her.

The murder shocked America in general and Hollywood in particular. Until then it was possible to see the shooting of John Lennon, nine years earlier, by Mark David Chapman, as a bizarre but isolated incident; Schaeffer's death suggested that, late in the 20th century, even a little fame could have tragic consequences.

"*I just want to
live like everyone
else, 'cause that's
what counts
in high school*"

Infected with HIV, he taught America a lesson in compassion

RYAN WHITE

1971–1990

He was just a kid from Kokomo, pretty much like any other, until a blood transfusion for his hemophilia at age 12 infected him with HIV. When Ryan White was diagnosed with AIDS in '84, some kids shunned him, and he was banned from middle school. He and his family successfully sued to have him readmitted, but the conflict had unleashed a wave of vitriol in the quiet Indiana town: Kids scribbled obscenities on his school locker, callers on radio talk shows labeled him "faggot," "homo" and "queer," and somebody slashed the tires on his family's car. After a bullet was fired through the Whites' living room window, the family decided to leave the town.

The heartbreaking story of Ryan White's persecution thrust him into the national spotlight; his guileless charm, and the power of his story, kept him there. Invited to speak on TV and in schools, he won over audiences with simple, honest answers to difficult questions. Do you cry, one woman asked? "I cry a lot for emotional reasons," he said. "Not for pain." Are you afraid of dying? "No. If I were worried about dying, I'd die. I'm not afraid, I'm just not ready yet. I want to go to Indiana University." What was it like in Kokomo? "[Kids would] run from me. Maybe I would have been afraid of AIDS too, but I wouldn't have been mean about it." Asked by a minister how his Christian faith had helped him cope, Ryan replied, "I've learned that God doesn't punish people. I've learned that God doesn't dislike homosexuals, like a lot of Christians think. AIDS isn't their fault, just like it isn't my fault."

Early on in the scourge of AIDS, Ryan White caused many Americans to reconsider what they had thought about the disease. "You're gonna do good for everybody who is sick," his mother, Jeanne, whispered to him as he lay dying. "It's a shame it has to be you." A few hours later she whispered, "Just let go, Ryan. It's time. Goodbye, buddy, goodbye, my pumpkin. I want to kiss you goodbye one more time." Moments later, the green dial on the heart monitor clicked off.

The quirky girl on that new sketch-comedy show became everybody's favorite Saturday-night date

GILDA RADNER

1946–1989

Lisa Loopner, Baba Wawa, Roseanne Roseannadanna, Emily Litella: Different characters, but all shared the same goofy, childlike DNA. "So much of what made up her characters didn't come of dreaming that stuff up," said a friend of *Saturday Night Live* star Gilda Radner. "They evolved from her being so open to the funniness in life." Said Anne Beatts, an early *SNL* writer: "If *Saturday Night Live* was like Never-Never-Land, the Island of Lost Boys, she was Tinker Bell. She just hadn't lost touch with the child in her."

She got her start, like so many *SNL* alumni, in Toronto's Second City comedy troupe. Producer Lorne Michaels recalled being impressed by such peculiar Radner abilities as "playing 14 Bingo cards at a time" or "remembering everything she'd eaten that day. She'd just literally reel it off—the french fries off someone else's plate, a Milk Dud from the bottom of her purse." When *SNL* premiered in 1975, "What Gilda Ate" became a regular segment.

Radner met Gene Wilder while making the 1982 film *Hanky Panky*. "There was a chemistry that was palpable," said a friend who visited the set. "They hadn't yet been together, but there was no chance that they weren't going to be." Wilder "was funny and handsome," Radner wrote. "And he smelled good." They married in 1984.

Two years later, Radner was diagnosed with ovarian cancer. For 2½ years, through 30 radiation treatments, she fought heroically. "My life had made me funny," Radner wrote in *It's Always Something,* her book about coping with the disease, "and cancer wasn't going to change that." Typically, she used her experience to help others. "I went bald because of chemotherapy," recalled Melinda Sheinkopf, a cancer survivor who had met Gilda. "She made it bearable. She brought me curlers, mousse and gel in a little bag. I laughed myself silly."

Radner lost her own battle, in her sleep, on May 20, 1989. She was 42.

*Children's television's
gentle genius walked
softly and let a
frog do the talking*

JIM HENSON

1936–1990

There may be no greater tribute to Jim Henson than this: Miss Piggy once danced *Swine Lake* with Rudolf Nureyev and, on another occasion, joined Beverly Sills to sing *Pigaletto*. Seldom, if ever, had so many stars—over the years, there were scores— been upstaged voluntarily by a pig.

That desire to join in the fun was testimony to the talent and sheer joy that radiated from Henson's most famous creations, *Sesame Street* and *The Muppets*. "Jim was an authentic American genius," said Children's Television Workshop's Joan Ganz Cooney. "He was our era's Charlie Chaplin, Mae West, W.C. Fields and Marx Brothers."

No one, Henson included, had any idea how sick he really was when he arrived at New York Hospital's emergency room on May 15, 1990. By then, doctors said, he was already in "acute respiratory distress," suffering from a virulent bacterial infection, heart and kidney failure and shock. He died within a day. "Possibly, had he been admitted earlier, something could have been done," said a hospital spokesman. Henson was 53.

Famously shy, Henson usually let his alter ego, Kermit the Frog, do the talking. The two were so closely linked that children, spotting Henson strolling in New York's Central Park, would shout out, "Look! There's Kermit!" Nothing, it seemed, pleased him more.

*Talent, looks, a
bright future—and
a fatal drug cocktail*

RIVER PHOENIX

1970–1993

One a.m., Oct. 31, 1993, the very first hour of Halloween day. Outside the Viper Room on L.A.'s Sunset Strip, witches milled with harlequins and a Louis XIV wannabe, and few paid much attention to the young man who lay on the sidewalk, thrashing spasmodically. It was, after all, West Hollywood. "It looked," said one witness, "like a normal occurrence."

The crowd would have paid more attention if they'd recognized the young man: River Phoenix, 23, star of *Stand by Me* and one of the hottest young actors in Hollywood. In jeans and sneakers, he looked like any young clubgoer who had knocked back too many or inhaled too much. But by the time an ambulance delivered him to Cedars-Sinai Medical Center at 1:34, he was in full cardiac arrest. At 1:51, River Phoenix was dead.

To many his death was doubly shocking: Not only *that* he had died, but how. A vegetarian and environmental activist, Phoenix didn't come across as a nightlife berserker. "I'm in shock," said his grandmother Margaret Dunetz. "I can't describe what a wonderful kid he is. I can't understand why—how—it could happen." Said Dan Mathews, director of International Campaigns for PETA: "The hardest drink I ever saw him drink was carrot juice."

But few people saw all sides of Phoenix; as he himself once remarked, "I have a lot of chameleon qualities—I get very absorbed in my surroundings." And although his background was colorful enough—raised by hippyish parents in an Oregon log cabin, he later moved with his family to Venezuela after his mother and father joined a religious cult—he seldom told his life story the same way twice. "I have lied and changed stories and contradicted myself left and right," he told a reporter days before his death, "so that at the end of the year you could read five different articles and say, 'This guy is schizophrenic.'"

An autopsy determined that Phoenix had died from "multiple drug intoxication," including heroin, cocaine and an over-the-counter cold medicine. Three years earlier, when his *Stand by Me* costar Corey Feldman was arrested for heroin possession, Phoenix gave a response that, later, would seem sadly prescient. "It makes you realize drugs aren't just done by bad guys and sleazebags," he said. "It's a universal disease."

A gentle man with a gift for comedy knew that he might die young

JOHN CANDY

1950–1994

It was after midnight, but John Candy was so excited he couldn't sleep. He called Richard Lewis and Robert Picardo, his costars in the movie *Wagons East,* to talk about scenes they'd filmed that day. "He was like a little kid who had a great day at camp," said Picardo. "He wanted to thank us."

Later that morning, Candy, 43, suffered a heart attack and died in his sleep. "Like the air has been sucked out of the world," said Eugene Levy, Candy's close friend and fellow *Second City TV* star, describing his feeling of loss. Levy was far from alone: Candy's humor and joy in living had brought him an army of friends; a meal at his home could be memorable. "John was always most relaxed when he was cooking," said Levy. "In fact, he was so relaxed that come 10 o'clock you'd realize John was just putting the turkey in the oven. You'd eat at 2 a.m., leave at 5 a.m., and later on you'd realize it was one of the greatest nights you ever had."

Food played a complex role in Candy's life, and, in all likelihood, in his death. His size—6'3" and 300 lbs., give or take—helped get him noticed, even in minor roles. "He doesn't add weight," *New Yorker* critic Pauline Kael wrote of his star-making turn in *Splash,* "he adds bounce and imagination." With encouragement from his *Summer Rental* director Carl Reiner, Candy entered the Pritikin Institute. He dropped 75 lbs. but found the regimen hard to maintain. "For a while he would eat nice," said Reiner, "but then he would say, 'Let's go have a bucket of shrimp.' He just couldn't resist." In the end, he may have felt a certain fatalism: Candy's father had died of heart problems at 35. "He felt he had inherited in his genes a Damoclean sword," said Reiner, "so it didn't matter what he did."

His funeral drew many friends—Martin Short, Tom Hanks, Chevy Chase, Bill Murray—who had helped shape comedy for a generation. "It hasn't sunk in," Levy said afterward. "We don't realize yet that John will be no more."

Here we are now, entertain us: A punk rocker recoils from the storm he helped create

KURT COBAIN

1967–1994

It could have been the pain in his stomach. Or the drugs. Or the crazy life he was leading. Most likely, it was all three.

On April 5, 1994, Kurt Cobain, 27, the "Smells Like Teen Spirit" singer and reluctant grunge icon, walked into the garage apartment of his Seattle home, placed his driver's license beside him—so there would be no question of identification—pointed a shotgun at himself and pulled the trigger. He had recently fled an L.A. drug-treatment center; his wife, musician Courtney Love, had been looking for him for days. A suicide note he left alluded to chronic, undiagnosed pains in his "burning, nauseous" stomach that had haunted him for years; heroin, he once said, was the only drug he had found that eased the pain. The shotgun blast was so fearsome that authorities had to use fingerprints to identify the body; Love later clipped and kept a lock of his blond hair.

Cobain, who grew up in the depressed logging town of Aberdeen, Wash., came by his alienation honestly. Two of his father's uncles had committed suicide in the '70s, and, said cousin Bev Cobain, a nurse, alcoholism and dysfunctional marriages plagued the clan. "I don't think there was much functional stuff going on in the whole family," she noted. A bright, hyperactive kid who had been prescribed Ritalin, Cobain "changed completely," said his mom, Wendy O'Connor, after his parents divorced when he was 8: "It just destroyed his life." He expressed his anger by drawing caricatures of his parents on his bedroom walls, labeling them "Dad sucks" and "Mom sucks."

What followed was a model rebellion: Uncontrollable, he was shuttled between his parents and relatives. At school he dyed his hair wild colors and taunted the jocks. "He stood out," said a friend, "like a turd in a punch bowl." He fell in love with punk music and picked up a guitar.

Despite having won two state art scholarships, Cobain decided to skip college for what he later called the "Aberdeen fantasy version of being a punk rocker." Days were spent drinking and drugging; he worked for a while as a janitor at his old high school and at one point lived under a bridge. He formed a band, Nirvana, and it began getting noticed. "You always went away hearing Kurt's voice," said Jack Endino, who later produced Nirvana's first album.

From Aberdeen, Nirvana moved on to Olympia and Seattle. Geffen Records signed the group in 1991; friends said Cobain never recovered from the shock when their breakthrough album, *Nevermind*, sold more than 10 million copies worldwide and gave Gen X an anthem, "Smells Like Teen Spirit." In front of cameras, he mugged with a madhouse gleam, acting as if only a demented world would declare him "the voice of a generation." Which, of course, only fed the legend. A saving grace was that he could, at times, laugh at the absurdity of it all. "Teenage angst has paid off well," he noted in one song, "Serve the Servants."

Cobain married Love in 1992, and the two had a daughter, Frances Bean, whom Kurt adored. But even his joy in fatherhood couldn't counter his demons. Why suicide? "It's complicated and hard to figure out," said Endino. "Basically, he was just a nice guy who didn't like fame. He was not your typical rock-star exhibitionist. . . . He was happy to be making music and to get the hell out of Aberdeen. But how many rock icons blow themselves away at the height of their fame?"

"Now he's gone and joined that stupid club"

—WENDY O'CONNOR, KURT'S MOM, ALLUDING TO THE PANTHEON OF ROCKERS WHO DIED YOUNG

Cobain, Love and Frances Bean posed on Sept. 2, 1993, six months before his death. Right: Nirvana's breakthrough *Nevermind* album—with its iconic photo— has sold more than 10 million copies.

*Dealt a catastrophic
blow, she responded
with passion and grace*

ELIZABETH GLASER

1947–1994

Elizabeth
Glaser with
Ariel, 2, ca.
1983. Ariel
died of AIDS
five years later.

It seemed like a tragedy beyond bearing, and she turned it into a gift. In 1981, when AIDS was little-known and less understood, Elizabeth Glaser, the wife of *Starsky and Hutch* actor Paul Michael Glaser, contracted HIV from a tainted blood transfusion; unwittingly, she passed it through breast milk to her newborn daughter Ariel (three years later her son Jake contracted the disease in utero). Elizabeth was diagnosed with AIDS in 1986; Ariel, age 7, died from it two years later. "After Ari died, I felt dead too," Elizabeth said. "I could no longer see any beauty in the world."

She could give up, or she could fight. She chose the latter. "She was a mother bear in that she had buried her daughter," said a friend. "Her efforts were all about trying to save her son. She felt that the next dollar spent or the next minute spent could be the moment of breakthrough." Glaser cofounded the Pediatric AIDS Foundation; in short order, her zeal, her connections and the blunt emotional power of her own story made PAF one of the most successful charities in Hollywood. Steven Spielberg donated $500,000 at the start, and annual fund-raising carnivals drew everyone from Jack Nicholson to Tom Cruise. "I think part of her appeal was that she was just a mother who happened to have two children with HIV," said actress Marlee Matlin. Donors were also moved by Glaser's passion. "Because Elizabeth lived on the edge, she was only interested in the truth," said actress Mary Steenburgen. "There wasn't one molecule of bulls--- in her."

"I have confronted my own fears, the fears of others, social discrimination and lack of education," Glaser said late in her own battle with AIDS. "It has now become a time in my life to learn about and understand death. If I can do that, it will truly be an achievement."

Elizabeth Glaser, 47, lost her battle on Dec. 3, 1994. Thanks to continued advances in HIV research, her son Jake is now 23 and a spokesman for what is now known as the Elizabeth Glaser Pediatric AIDS Foundation.

*An angry employee, a
gun, and heartbreak*

SELENA

1971–1995

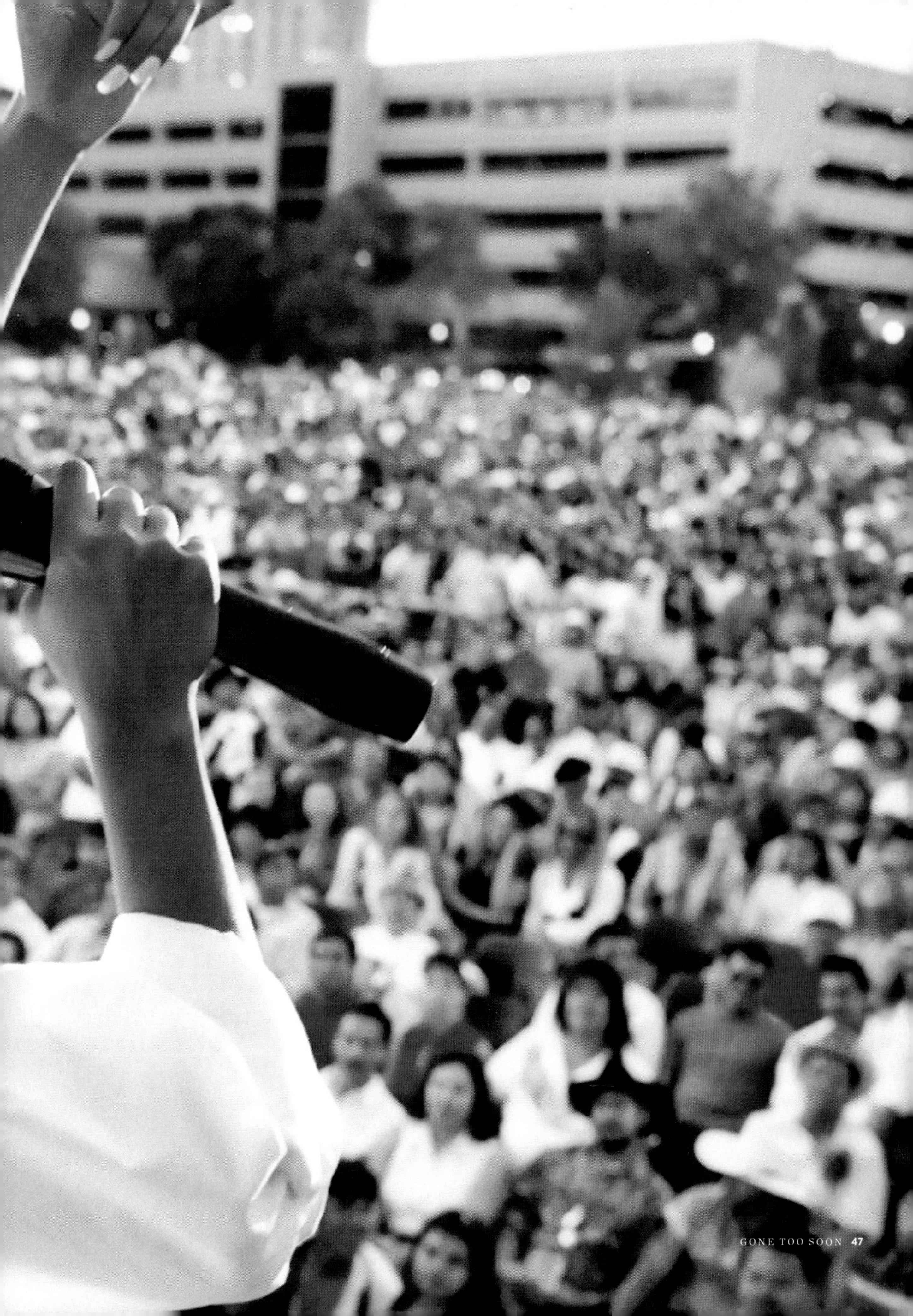

"She was sexy like Madonna, but never vulgar," said a friend. "Her sweetness came through"

Yolanda Saldivar (with Selena in 1995) founded the singer's fan club and helped run her clothing business.

Grief-stricken, fans by the thousands converged on Corpus Christi, Texas, to leave flowers and pay their respects.

Selena had touched them in life; now, as many as 50,000 mourners, from as far away as Canada and Guatemala, converged on Corpus Christi, Texas, to pay their respects. Their sense of loss—and denial—was overwhelming. At one point a rumor swept the crowd that Selena Quintanilla-Perez, 23, the Queen of Tejano music, was still alive and that her coffin, surrounded by white long-stemmed roses, was empty. Finally, her family ordered the coffin opened briefly to confirm the unacceptable truth. There she lay, her lips and long nails done in bloodred, wearing a purple gown.

The bizarre tragedy unfolded two days before, on March 31, 1995, when Selena went to a local Days Inn to confront Yolanda Saldivar, 34, the former president of her fan club. Suspected by Selena and her family of embezzling funds, Saldivar was on the verge of being fired and knew it. Soon after Selena arrived, Saldivar shot her once in the back with a .38 revolver. The singer staggered to the lobby before collapsing and being rushed to a hospital. Saldivar kept SWAT teams at bay for nearly 10 hours as she sat in a pickup truck with a gun to her head, threatening suicide, before finally surrendering.

For Selena's family, who knew Saldivar well, the rush of events had a surreal quality. "The ultimate sorrow a human can feel is when someone dies," said her father, Abraham Quintanilla Jr. "I felt like this was all a dream."

For Latin music enthusiasts, the most apt comparison was with the death of John Lennon. Selena was vastly talented and deeply adored. In recent years she had played to audiences of up to 80,000; her most recent album, *Amor Prohibido*, sold more than 500,000 copies and received a Grammy nomination. Said one critic: "We will never know how far she could have gone."

Saldivar, a loner, had founded Selena's fan club and become close to the star; Saldivar's home, said an acquaintance, was a virtual shrine to the singer. Said Esmeralda Garza, the fan club's former secretary: "She probably couldn't accept the fact that she wasn't going to be around Selena anymore."

At her trial, Saldivar claimed the shooting was accidental. She was convicted of first-degree murder and sentenced to life in prison.

Equal parts musician and mellow ringmaster, he kept the '60s alive for 30 years

JERRY GARCIA

1942–1995

Bearded and gray in his later years, a middle-aged man whose weight sometimes ballooned to 300 lbs., Jerry Garcia seemed the antithesis of a rock star. His idea of stage craft was to stand rock-still and utter not a word to the multitudes who adored him. Yet he was a riveting performer, a benevolent Buddha whose face beamed with merriment and sometimes sorrow as notes cascaded from a custom guitar he seemed to play not with his hands but with his heart. "For me," he said, "it's always emotional."

On Aug. 9, 1995, Garcia's heart, 53 years old and ravaged by years of drug use and related health problems, gave out. The leader of the Grateful Dead was found during a routine bed check at a California drug treatment center, where he had checked in after a relapse into heroin addiction. An autopsy attributed his death not to drugs but to acute hardening of the arteries. "He created an entire subculture," said Chris Hillman, one the of the founders of the Byrds. "He had his roots in bluegrass and blues and folk, and he was able to take that and make this eclectic mixture of sounds, always delving into more experimental things. He was a true musical explorer."

A Pied Piper, too: As the '60s hippie culture faded, Garcia, as much as anyone, continued to hold its rainbow banner aloft, lurching forward through the decades, laughing much of the way. "It's not just music, it's a religion," said San Francisco poet Hugh Romney, better known as the cosmic clown Wavy Gravy, of the Dead's music and movable-feast concerts. "The beauty of the Grateful Dead was their relationship with their fans. They just take this great big ball of love and bounce it out to the fans, and the fans bounce it back, and each time it just gets bigger." Garcia called the Deadheads—ardent, tie-dyed fans who followed the band from city to city, camping in stadium parking lots—"this time-frame's version of the archetypal American adventure. It used to be that you could run away and join the circus . . . or ride the freight trains."

That unique sense of community made Grateful Dead shows a cultural phenomenon: During the three years before Garcia's death, the band grossed $162 million. "When we get onstage," he once said, "we really want to be transformed from ordinary players to extraordinary ones, like forces of a larger consciousness. So maybe it's that seat-of-the-pants shamanism that keeps the audience coming back and keeps it fascinating for us too."

An innocent who jumped head-first into the disco whirl, Ernest Hemingway's granddaughter never quite regained her footing

MARGAUX HEMINGWAY

1955–1996

"I was basically a little s--- in cowboy boots going 'Yippie skippie' and 'Yahoo!' with a big grin," Margaux Hemingway recalled of an early trip to New York City at age 19. The small-town routine—Hemingway hailed from Ketchum, Idaho, where her famous grandfather, Ernest, had lived—proved irresistible to at least one man: Errol Wetson, 33, a hamburger-chain heir and entrepreneur who spotted her at the Plaza Hotel's Palm Court, grabbed a bottle of champagne and a rose and knocked on the door of her suite. Said Hemingway: "I fell in love."

She moved in with Wetson, who introduced her to people who could help the fresh-faced six-footer launch a modeling career. Within a year she was on the cover of *Vogue* and even Time—and hanging out with Halston and Liza Minnelli at Studio 54. She loved the nightlife but felt like a fraud. "To me they were the real celebrities, and I was just a girl from Idaho," she said. To banish anxiety, she turned to alcohol.

As quickly as glory came, it began to slip maddeningly away. Her marriage ended; her would-be breakout movie, *Lipstick,* garnered more attention for her 14-year-old sister Mariel. Margaux moved to Paris with a Venezuelan movie director and spent herself into serious debt. "Margaux would talk very loudly about things you don't normally hear in polite society," recalled a Paris socialite.

By 1994 the former supermodel was searching and hoping. She had spent time at the Betty Ford Center and studied shamanism and philosophy with American Indians and Hawaiian kahunas. "I needed to go inside and clear the blockages," she said, "because nothing was coming to me, no jobs, no work."

In June 1996, pals noticed that Hemingway seemed depressed. When she dropped from sight for a week, one concerned friend drove to Margaux's modest Santa Monica apartment and, peering inside, saw her body, lying in bed. Hemingway, 41, had taken an overdose of phenobarbital. "It's very difficult when people don't want you anymore," said Caren Elin, a longtime friend. "She was just a gentle, loving soul who got lost in fame and fortune."

A child murdered at Christmastime. Far from open and shut, the case may stay open . . . forever

JONBENET RAMSEY

1990–1996

As Patsy Ramsey later told authorities, she walked downstairs to make coffee on Dec. 26, 1996, and discovered a note, neatly hand-printed, claiming that her daughter JonBenét, 6, had been kidnapped and demanding a ransom of $118,000. Patsy said she ran to her daughter's room, found the bed empty, let out a scream and phoned police. Hours later, as the family and investigators waited for a call from the alleged kidnappers, Patsy's husband, John, began a search of the Boulder, Colo., home and found JonBenét, her mouth taped shut and a cord around her neck, dead in a basement room.

John and Patsy drew suspicion when both hired criminal lawyers and initially refused to be formally interviewed by police. Neither was ever charged with a crime, and Patsy died of cancer at 49 in 2006. The arrest of a suspect, John Mark Karr, in Thailand became an embarrassment when his confession was nullified by DNA evidence, and the case became, again, what it had been for a decade: one of America's greatest unsolved mysteries.

Said one admirer: "He made clothes for women who want to walk into a room and have people say, 'Wow!'"

GIANNI VERSACE

1946–1997

Ten years later, it still makes no sense. Gianni Versace, supernova of Italian design, stopped at a café, bought a handful of magazines and strolled back to Casa Casuarina, the elegant palazzo he called home in Miami. As he opened the front gate, a young man stepped up and shot him twice in the head.

The killer's identity proved almost as shocking as the crime: Andrew Cunanan, 27, was 2½ months into a bizarre killing spree that had landed him on the FBI's 10 Most Wanted list. A high-priced prostitute who lived off wealthy older men, Cunanan had murdered David Madson, 33, an architect, and Jeffrey Trail, 28, in Minnesota; Chicago millionaire Lee Miglin, 72; and cemetery caretaker William Reese, 45, in New Jersey. Police found Reese's stolen red pickup truck blocks from Versace's villa; eight days later, as they closed in on a Miami houseboat where Cunanan was thought to be hiding, he shot himself in the head.

Although there was some evidence that victim and killer may have met at some time in their lives, Versace, 50, most likely died because he represented everything Cunanan desperately wanted. "I think he looked at Versace as a symbolic victim," said former FBI agent Robert K. Ressler. "Versace represented and stood for power, wealth, fame, celebrity, flamboyant lifestyle—everything Cunanan worshipped and aspired to."

Versace built that life from nothing. The son of a seamstress and an appliance salesman from dirt-poor Reggio di Calabria in southern Italy, he designed his first gown at 9—a one-shouldered, black-velvet affair—and launched himself toward the stratosphere with a collection under his own name in 1978. Mixing elegance and shock value—he once described himself as "half royalty and half rock and roll"—he became a favorite of celebrities from Princess Di to Madonna and amassed a fortune estimated at $800 million. Though mindful of money's limitations—"I prefer a happy vulgar person to an unhappy chic person," he once said—he delighted in those things that money *could* buy. "It was lavish beyond belief," fashion journalist Michael Gross recalled of a visit to Versace's 17th-century Milan palazzo. "A room full of antique globes, every single one of them beautiful objects. Waiters everywhere, champagne flowing and pieces of furniture so deep your legs didn't reach the edge if you leaned back. He was playing out a dream of wealth beyond measure. . . . It's like the Sun King. He reflected light on to those around him, and they in turn reflected back upon him."

*Around the world, millions
mourned Princess Diana,
the woman they loved*

PRINCESS
DIANA

1961–1997

Early on the evening of Aug. 30, 1997, Princess Diana telephoned the *Daily Mail*'s Richard Kay, one of the reporters who often wrote about her. She was, he said later, "as happy as I have ever known her. For the first time in years, all was well with her world." After the drawn-out drama of her rocky marriage and headline-making divorce, she had begun a new life and, for the first time, she was publicly dating: In the space of five weeks, she had gone on three vacations with Dodi Al Fayed, 42, son of billionaire Mohamed Al Fayed.

That night, in Paris, Diana and Dodi ate a late dinner at the Ritz Hotel's L'Espadon restaurant. "They looked like two love-struck teenagers," said a Ritz staffer.

At about 11:15, the maître d' whispered that about 30 paparazzi were massed outside the hotel. Minutes later Dodi's Range Rover, with his chauffeur at the wheel, sped away from the hotel—but it was only a decoy, and few of the photographers were fooled. Resigned to running the gauntlet themselves, Diana and Dodi, at about 12:15 a.m., climbed into a Mercedes-Benz S 280 driven by Henri Paul, the hotel's assistant director of security, and raced from the hotel toward Dodi's apartment, with the paparazzi in hot pursuit. On an expressway along the Seine, Paul picked up speed and entered the Alma tunnel.

Then it happened: "There was this huge, violent, terrifying crash followed by the lone sound of a car horn," said a man who had been near the tunnel entrance.

Racing at an estimated 121 mph, Paul lost control on a slight curve; the Mercedes hurtled head-on into a concrete column, rolled over, hit a wall and came to rest, upright, facing oncoming traffic. Paul, whose blood was later found to contain triple France's legal alcohol limit, and Dodi were dead at the scene; bodyguard Trevor Rees-Jones, the only one wearing a seat belt, was injured but alive. Unconscious, Princess Diana was rushed to a hospital, but doctors could do nothing about her massive internal bleeding. A Palace official announced her death at 4:57 a.m.

Her funeral, five days later in London, drew the largest television audience in history, about 2 billion. The grief-stricken populace piled flowers several feet deep in front of Kensington Palace; thousands of mourners observed the 2-mile march to Westminster Abbey. Many waited through the night in chilly, rainy weather. "One night is nothing after all she gave us," said one Londoner. Of the funeral procession itself—Diana's flag-draped coffin, on a gun

When Charles proposed, Diana responded, "Yes, please." Their 1981 wedding drew a TV audience of 700 million.

Diana's brother Earl Spencer and Princes William, Harry and Charles watched her casket leave Westminster Abbey. Right: a bouquet from Harry.

carriage, followed by Princes Charles, William and Harry, members of the royal family and, in a fitting touch, more than 500 workers and beneficiaries from charities Di had helped—was heartbreaking. Said supermarket worker Jason Fryer, 28: "Soon as the first horse come around the corner, the lump in your throat got so big you couldn't possibly have no other emotions."

As the gun carriage passed the Queen, who stood at the gate of Buckingham Palace, she bowed her head—a sensational gesture written in no book of protocol. "It was a lovely gesture," said royals expert Brian Hoey. The royal family "had little love for her, but the Queen was recognizing the affection and respect she was held in by the people."

Diana was laid to rest on a small island on her family's Althorp estate. "Diana was out to make a mark and she did," said a mourner at Kensington Palace. "She conquered the world."

An upbeat troubadour sang of a mythical mountain world and sometimes struggled in the real one

JOHN DENVER

1943–1997

He was something of a paradox: His folksy lyrics sang of blue skies and quiet mountain streams; in real life, he had been through two divorces, admitted to infidelities and had DWI problems. Some critics found his music saccharine; 13 platinum albums, including *Back Home Again* and *Rocky Mountain High* and nearly 20 TV specials made clear he touched millions. "Some of my songs are about very simple things," he said. "But those simple things are meaningful to me and have obviously meant something to people all over the world, even if it's in a karaoke bar."

Denver, 53, had taken up flying in part to heal a fractious relationship with his father, a test pilot. "It was his approval I most wanted," Denver said. Highly experienced, he nonetheless ran into trouble while flying near Monterey, Calif. "He banked to one side, with the right wing down, the left wing up," said a witness. "I thought he was a stunt pilot. Then he hit the water." Investigators later determined that Denver, insufficiently familiar with his new airplane, probably lost control while trying to solve a fuel problem.

A TV sitcom, a real-life murder

PHIL HARTMAN

1948–1998

Despite surface appearances, it had been a volatile marriage. He was friendly and famously easygoing in public, reclusive when he got home. She was beautiful, insecure and prone to high drama. "I go into my cave," *Saturday Night Live* and *NewsRadio* star Phil Hartman once said by way of describing his marriage to Brynn, "and she throws grenades to get me out."

The evening of May 27 started with yet another argument. According to friends, Brynn, 40, who had struggled with alcohol and cocaine in the past, had recently slipped back into bad habits; Phil, said his friend Steven Small, "made it very clear that if she started using drugs again, that would end the relationship." The couple's arguments, noted Small, usually followed a familiar pattern: "When she got amped up, he would simply go to sleep. He would withdraw. And in the morning he'd wake up, and everything would be fine."

Not this time. Shortly before 3 a.m., Brynn shot Hartman, 49, three times as he slept, twice in the head and once in the side, with a .38-cal. handgun he usually kept in a safe. Afterward she fled to the home of longtime friend Ron Douglas and confessed. Unsure whether to believe her, he followed her back to the Hartmans' L.A. home and called 911. Police arrived within minutes; as they were escorting the couple's daughter Birgen, 6, to safety, while son Sean, 9, waited outside, officers heard another gunshot. Storming the bedroom, they found Phil Hartman's body on the bed; next to it, with a single gunshot wound to her head, lay Brynn.

"This is just a tragedy beyond description," said Rita Wilson, Tom Hanks's wife and Hartman's costar in the 1996 film *Jingle All the Way*. "Now two children are left without the two most important people in their lives, and with a lifetime of confusion." (As provided in the couple's wills, both children would be cared for by Brynn's married sister in Wisconsin.) "They always seemed happy," said a bartender at one of their favorite restaurants, where the pair had recently celebrated Brynn's birthday. "They always held hands and laughed and seemed like they were having a good time."

One year after the murder, Gregory Omdahl, Brynn's brother and the executor of the Hartman estate, sued the makers of Zoloft, claiming the psychoactive drug, which Brynn had been taking, had played a role in her rampage. The suit was settled out of court in 2001; no details were made public.

According to a source close to the family, Sean, 9 (right, with his parents and sister Birgen in 1995), told police he'd heard sounds "like the slamming of a door"—the first shots fired by Brynn.

Fueled by drugs, the cute kid from Diff'rent Strokes *disappeared into a long tunnel with no exit*

DANA PLATO

1964–1999

Diff'rent Strokes folks (clockwise from far left): Plato, Coleman, Bain, Bridges.

Sadly, although she starred on a hit sitcom for six years, Dana Plato may be best remembered for a brief performance in a Las Vegas video store in 1991. She walked in, pointed a pellet gun at a cashier and demanded money. After handing over $164, the clerk called 911 and reported, "I've just been robbed by the girl who played Kimberly on *Diff'rent Strokes.*"

In the depressing world of troubled child actors, Plato helped define the modern template. She began acting at 6 and had appeared in some 250 commercials before being cast at 13 in *Strokes.* And then: At 14, according to her manager at the time, she overdosed on Valium; by 15, she was coming to the set drunk; at 18, she got pregnant and was dropped from the show. She seemed not to care. She told Conrad Bain, who played *Strokes*' bemused and tolerant dad, Mr. Drummond, "When I get the baby, I will never be alone again."

Five years after the baby, Tyler, was born, custody was awarded to his father. Short of cash and plagued by substance abuse, Plato robbed the video store. (Wayne Newton, who had never met Plato but felt sorry for her, posted her $13,000 bail.) Later that year she was arrested twice for forging Valium prescriptions. Somewhere along the way she posed for *Playboy* and appeared in a soft-core porn flick, *Different Strokes: The Story of Jack and Jill . . . and Jill.*

The drugs never seemed to go away. Paul Petersen, who as a child costarred on *The Donna Reed Show,* recalled appearing on *Sally Jessy Raphael* with Plato in 1990. "She bumped into me, fresh out of the bathroom, with cocaine powder all over her nose," he said. "Five minutes later she was on the air saying she's clean and sober. She lied to everybody."

She could also be wryly charming. Her *Strokes* costars Gary Coleman and Todd Bridges famously made headlines of their own. The show's creative supervisor, Al Burton, remembers meeting Plato at a party: "She told me, 'I just posed nude for *Playboy,* Gary is suing his parents, Todd was arrested. That Drummond sure was a terrible father.'"

On May 7, 1999, Plato, 34, appeared on Howard Stern's radio show, where her history prompted a number of cruel jokes. The next day her new boyfriend, Robert Menchaca, awoke to find her unconscious in her 37-ft. Winnebago, which was parked outside his parents' house in Moore, Okla. His mother, a nurse technician, helped perform CPR, to no avail. The medical examiner ruled her death—from an overdose of a muscle relaxant and Lortab, a powerful painkiller—a suicide.

Blessed and burdened at birth, he responded with grace and self-deprecating wit

JOHN F. KENNEDY JR.

1960–1999

On a business trip to Toronto five days before his death, John F. Kennedy Jr. was hobbling around on a left ankle broken in a recent paragliding accident. His crutches scarcely slowed him down. Keith Stein, a Toronto businessman who had helped broker a meeting with a potential investor in Kennedy's *George* magazine, marveled at his guest's energy. "He was sticking his head out the car window all the time," said Stein, "curious about everything." When it was time to leave, Kennedy, who had flown in on his private plane from Martha's Vineyard, Mass., with a flight instructor, talked about his love of flying. He lamented that on the trip back to New York he wouldn't have a chance to fly at night, which he especially enjoyed because of the navigation challenges.

Kennedy always exhibited a healthy skepticism about the mythology surrounding his family, yet with his natural passion, daring and style, he effortlessly seemed to embody it. When the single-engine Piper Saratoga II that he was piloting plunged into the ocean off Martha's Vineyard on the night of July 16, 1999, killing Kennedy, 38, his wife, Carolyn Bessette Kennedy, 33, and her sister Lauren Bessette, 34, it seemed impossible that a life lived so vibrantly could so suddenly end. Across the nation, indeed the world, stricken citizens anxiously monitored the deluge of television, radio and print coverage of the tragedy. On vacation in the Alps, Pope John Paul II sent word he was saying a prayer for the families.

Kennedy had been flying to Martha's Vineyard nearly every weekend that summer, staying with Carolyn at the 375-acre estate he had inherited with his sister Caroline Kennedy Schlossberg after the death of their mother, Jacqueline Kennedy Onassis, in 1994. Around the island John, especially, was a familiar figure, often Rollerblading or riding his bike along the narrow roads or cruising in his beloved vintage Pontiac GTO convertible. Three years earlier he had bought his first aircraft, a two-cylinder ultralight, essentially a seat with a propeller and wings attached, that startled his neighbors. "They didn't know what it was," said one local. "It made this weird noise, like a flying lawn mower. But he really seemed excited about it, because he was always in it."

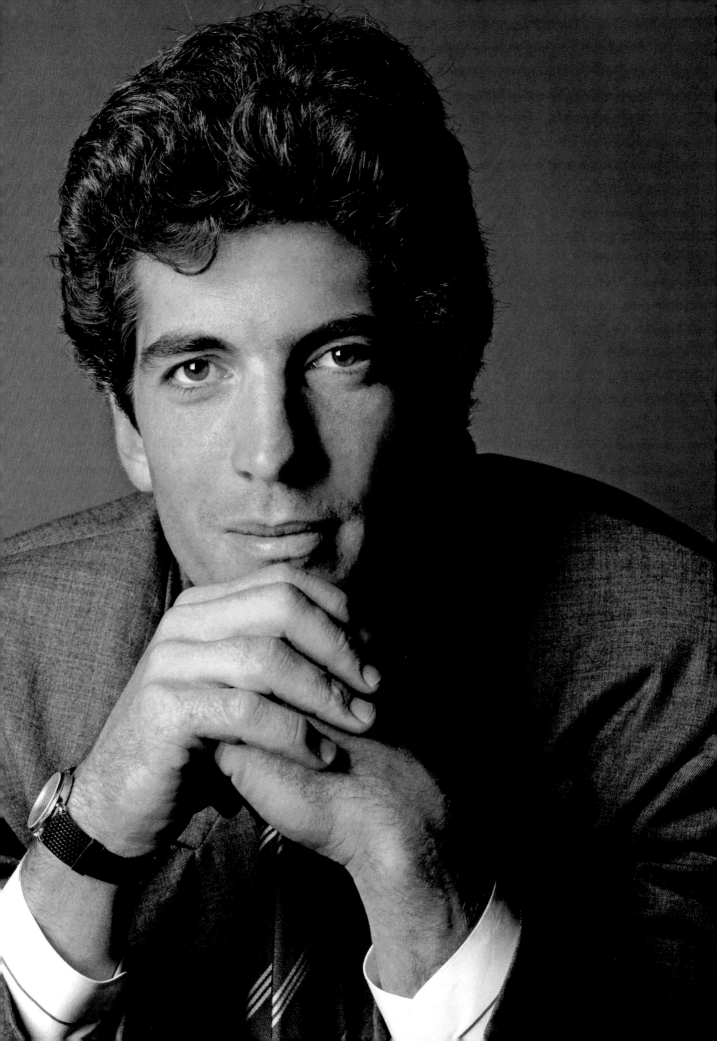

"It's hard for me to talk about a legacy. We're a family like any other"

President Kennedy was killed a few weeks after this famous Oval Office photo was taken.

"They had their own special brand of magic," Sen. Ted Kennedy said of John and Carolyn.

His interest only grew. Kennedy went on to get a basic pilot's license, which allowed him to fly in good visibility, and was working toward an instrument rating, which would let him fly at night or in bad weather. He kept his plane, a six-seater he bought used for an estimated $300,000, at New Jersey's Essex County Airport. "He was just one of the guys," said the owner of the local flight school. "He'd hang out like everybody else and talk about flying."

On July 16 Kennedy took off from runway 22 at 8:38 p.m., just after sunset, and headed northeast. At the time, a heat wave had left skies so hazy that one Essex pilot had scrubbed his own plan to fly to the Vineyard. Visibility was somewhere between five and eight miles—within visual flight rules, but hardly ideal conditions. Still, said a charter pilot who knew Kennedy, "he was smart enough to know his limitations."

Kennedy apparently took his usual route to the Vineyard, hugging the Connecticut coastline at 5,500 feet before heading east to cross 30 miles of ocean. He did not contact any of the control towers along the way to get weather updates. At about 9:30 a blip on a radar screen, later determined to be Kennedy's plane, began behaving erratically: descending quickly and turning right, then rising again and turning left. Then it plunged, dropping at nearly eight times the normal rate of descent, and disappeared.

Dr. Bob Arnot, then an NBC medical correspondent, had been flying his own private plane in the area a half hour earlier. At one point, he said later, he hit a wall of haze that obscured everything around him, including the horizon, and he was forced to rely on instruments. "I haven't been in conditions like that for years," said Arnot. "I have 5,000 hours, and I had a problem. At 100 hours of flying [experience], I would have been very worried."

The National Transportation Safety Board later determined that, in fading light and with the horizon disappearing, Kennedy had become disoriented and lost control.

"John and Carolyn are true soulmates," said her father, mother and stepfather in a joint statement. ". . . We take solace in the thought that they will comfort Lauren for eternity." In 2001 Carolyn and Lauren's mother, Ann Freeman, reached a financial settlement with John's estate; details were kept confidential.

A beloved actor,
a beautiful day—
and, without
warning, tragedy

JOHN RITTER

1948–2003

Fresh from a workout with his trainer, John Ritter arrived on the Disney lot at 11:30 a.m., bumped into actor Howard Alonzo and gave him a bear hug. The star of the ABC sitcom *8 Simple Rules for Dating My Teenage Daughter,* Ritter was in a great mood: It was his daughter Stella's first week in preschool, and he was getting a kick out of being her personal chauffeur.

On the set he said he felt tired. He went to his dressing room to rest but began sweating and vomiting. A studio doctor told him to go the hospital immediately.

The situation got worse, quickly: Doctors detected a tear in his main artery and sent him to surgery. He died on the operating table shortly after 10 p.m.

His death shocked fans and devastated many in Hollywood. By all accounts, Ritter, 54, was as personable and funny offscreen as the characters he played on TV—thanks, perhaps, to the fact that he himself was the son of two modest, down-home stars: Tex Ritter, a B-western personality and country singer, and Dorothy Fay, at one time the Grand Ole Opry's official greeter. "When I saw his picture on the TV screen with two dates on it," said actress Markie Post, a friend, "it was like a kick in the gut."

"He was a ridiculously proud father," said Joyce DeWitt, one of Ritter's costars on *Three's Company,* the '70s sitcom that made them both famous. (In addition to Stella, with second wife Amy Yasbeck, Ritter had three children with his first wife, actress Nancy Morgan.) His marriage to Yasbeck was "magical," said Post. "They were like the perfect comedy team with love mixed in."

Friends say he realized his life had been blessed in many ways and was grateful. "John was never happier than the day he died," said one. "Everything was perfect."

1961-2006

"You're still you," she
said after his accident.
"And I love you"

CHRISTOPHER & DANA REEVE

1952–2004

Dana Reeve was performing in a play in Costa Mesa, Calif., when the call came. "She was trembling, but she stayed focused," said Mimi Lieber, another actress in the cast. "She asked, 'Do I need to get a plane?' And the nurse on the phone said yes. She asked, 'Could he die?' And the nurse said yes. And then she asked, 'Do I need to call the kids?' And the nurse said yes."

Dana Reeve raced home to Connecticut, where her husband, actor Christopher Reeve, 52, paralyzed in a riding accident a decade before, had been hospitalized after developing a sudden, raging infection. At 5:20 p.m. the next day, his family gathered around him, his heart gave out. "I think," said Lieber, "he waited for her."

Christopher had been a strapping, 6'4" leading man, the star of four *Superman* movies, before crushed vertebrae cost him almost all feeling below his neck and tethered him to a respirator. He later said that he thought of letting go of life altogether, until Dana uttered the words that saved him: "You're still you, and I love you." Together they built a brave new life, focused on their young son Will and, through the Christopher Reeve Paralysis Foundation, on raising millions for spinal cord research and helping others in the same situation. "Chris had far greater challenges than I've faced, and faced them with courage, intelligence and dignity I can only aspire to," said his friend Michael J. Fox, who has Parkinson's disease. "If he could ever have walked, he would have walked over to help someone else get up." What *did* upset Reeve? "I get pretty impatient," he once said, "with people who are able-bodied but are somehow paralyzed for other reasons."

Tragically, even after Christopher's death, more heartbreak followed: Nine months later, Dana was diagnosed with lung cancer. She fought bravely, spoke publicly and did everything in her power to comfort and provide for Will, 13. (He would later move in with family friends.) She died, age 44, 17 months after Christopher. "Her compassion, her fortitude are a source of inspiration," said a friend. "Her impact is immeasurable."

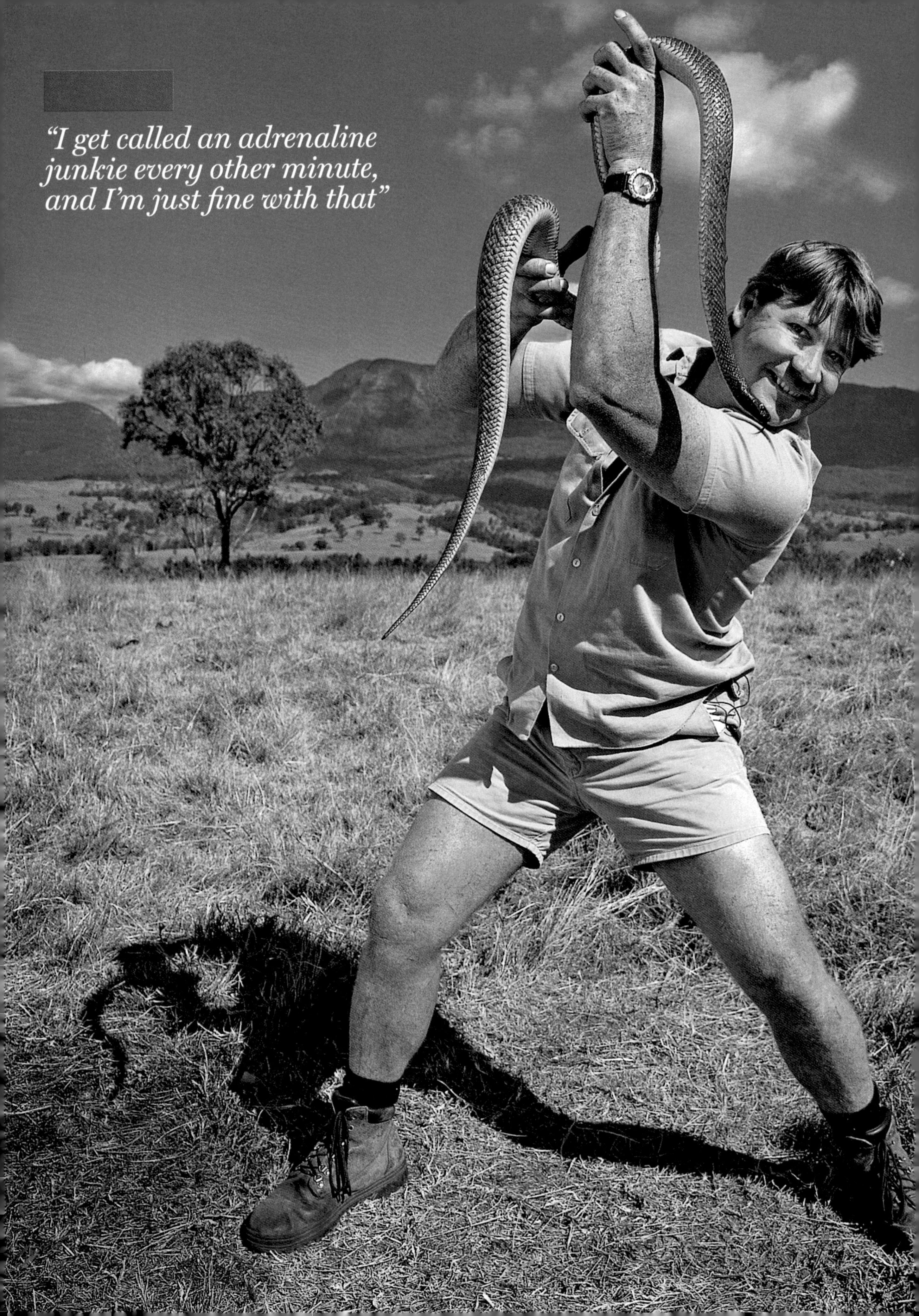

"I get called an adrenaline junkie every other minute, and I'm just fine with that"

*For TV's croc hunter,
death came out of the blue*

STEVE IRWIN

1962–2006

Anchored off Australia's Great Barrier Reef in 2006, Crocodile Hunter Steve Irwin decided to film a segment for his daughter Bindi's upcoming wildlife show on the Discovery Kids channel. "He was in such a good frame of mind," said longtime friend John Stainton. "We sat together in the early hours, 5 a.m., 6 a.m, having a cup of tea, just talking about how good life was."

Irwin, 44, slipped into the water with his cameraman to film a school of stingrays, docile creatures who usually tolerate visitors. Then it happened. As Irwin snorkeled above a bull ray, it stopped, then whipped its razor-sharp tail directly up toward Irwin and plunged the barb deep into his chest, piercing his heart.

Irwin pulled the barb out himself, and crewmen quickly hauled him aboard his boat. But there was no way to stop the bleeding. "He pulled the barb out," said Stainton, "and the next minute he's gone. That was it."

Irwin's Animal Planet adventure shows, including *The Crocodile Hunter* and *Croc Files,* had made him a familiar figure to kids and their parents around the world; in Australia, where he was something of a national mascot, the prime minister offered to hold a state funeral. Said actor Russell Crowe, a friend: "He touched my heart. I believed in him."

Slowly recovering from the tragedy, Irwin's American-born wife, Terri, 42, took up the job of continuing the family's Australia Zoo, on the country's Queensland coast; daughter Bindi's show, *Bindi the Jungle Girl,* began airing in June 2007.

A small-town girl from Texas led a life made for the tabloids

ANNA NICOLE SMITH

1967–2007

In the end, it was a sad circus, a perfect storm of drugs, paternity claims, contested wills, tabloid headlines, a motherless child and Zsa Zsa Gabor's eighth husband, Prince Frederic von Anhalt. Stories about the death of Anna Nicole Smith likened it to that of her idol, Marilyn Monroe—two buxom platinum blondes who'd come to Hollywood, found fame and died young. It was, of course, a facile comparison: Monroe's life had featured real glamour, memorable movies—*Bus Stop, Some Like It Hot*—and an all-star cast that included Joe DiMaggio, Arthur Miller and Robert Kennedy. Anna Nicole Smith was famous mostly for trying very hard to be famous, from *Playboy* covers to her 2002 E! reality series, *The Anne Nicole Show*. Her manager/lover/publicist/caretaker, lawyer Howard K. Stern, 38, was many things, but he was, certainly, no Jack Kennedy.

The end probably began shortly after the Texas-born Smith, 39, gave birth to a daughter, Dannielynn, on Sept. 7, 2006, in the Bahamas. Days later her son Daniel, 20, who had been visiting, died of what doctors determined was a combination of antidepressants and methadone. Smith was devastated; simultaneously, she was forced to cope with a newborn, mourn her son, battle a paternity suit from former lover Larry Birkhead, 34, who claimed to be Dannielynn's dad (so, among others, did Frederick von Anhalt), and a fight over ownership of the Bahamas house she was living in.

On Feb. 5 Smith checked into the Seminole Hard Rock Hotel & Casino in Hollywood, Fla. "She seemed a little woozy," said a witness who saw her in the lobby. "She was walking straight but was being held up by Howard." Three days later, her nurse found her unconscious in her room; emergency personnel couldn't revive her, and she died shortly after arriving at Memorial Regional Hospital. An autopsy found that she had died of an accidental overdose of prescription drugs.

After months of legal maneuvering and headline-producing hearings, Birkhead, a photographer, was determined to be the father of Dannielynn and granted custody. Ex-boyfriend Stern will remain the executor of Smith's will. The fate of Smith's decade-long suit against the estate of J. Howard Marshall, II—the Texas billionaire she married when she was 26 and he was 89—of which Dannielynn could be a beneficiary, remains unresolved.

ENTERTAINERS

*A rocket ride to stardom hid
a talented comedian's troubled
psyche and cries for help*

FREDDIE PRINZE

1954–1977

In 1973 he was in high school. In 1974 he was starring on a hit NBC series, *Chico and the Man*. It all happened at warp speed, and it may have twisted Freddie Prinze.

Not that there hadn't been substantial turbulence already. The son of immigrants—his father was Hungarian and part Jewish, his mother Puerto Rican and Catholic—he grew up working-class in New York City and jokingly described himself as "Hungarican." "I fitted in nowhere," he told *Rolling Stone*. "I wasn't true spic, true Jew, true anything. I was a miserable fat schmuck kid with glasses and asthma." Like many comedians, he learned to use humor as a shield; when his parents sent him to a Lutheran school, he said, "all was confusing, until I found out I could crack up the priest doing Martin Luther."

His talent got him into Manhattan's High School of Performing Arts, which he attended when he wasn't too exhausted from performing, often for free, at late-night comedy clubs. In 1973 he appeared on a show with Jack Paar after a talent scout caught his act. That led to a spot on *The Tonight Show Starring Johnny Carson*, which led to a producer casting him in *Chico and the Man*, a sitcom about a crusty white auto mechanic and his wisecracking Chicano assistant. (When the sitcom became a huge hit, Chicanos—Americans of Mexican descent—protested the use of Prinze, a New York Puerto Rican, to portray one of their own. "If I can't play a Chicano because I'm Puerto Rican," Prinze observed, "then God's really gonna be mad when he finds out Charlton Heston played Moses.")

But the jokes, as always, hid trouble. Friends would later recall that Prinze, as a child, could often be moody. He had, said his publicist, "fits of elation and fits of depression." Overwhelmed by the demands of his new life and by his own troubled psyche, he wallowed in drugs, and an impulsive marriage imploded, painfully, after about a year. Distraught, he told friends he was going to shoot himself; few believed him. On Jan. 28, 1977, in front of his manager, he did. "He was in turmoil, he was suffering such pain," his friend, entertainer Tony Orlando, said at his funeral. "And yet his audience never knew."

He was 22.

Stricken with AIDS, the Midnight Express *star hoped his death would sound a warning*

BRAD DAVIS

1949–1991

In 1985, while rehearsing the play *The Normal Heart,* in which he portrayed an AIDS activist, Brad Davis had a chilling premonition. "The cast spent time with AIDS patients," playwright Larry Kramer recalled, "and one of them talked about drug-use transmission. Later, Brad told me a little bell went off in his head, and he thought, 'Uh-oh, I hope I'll be okay.'"

Later that year, Davis, a popular actor best known for his starring role in the prison-escape drama *Midnight Express,* donated blood and received notification that he was HIV positive. He believed he had contracted the virus through IV drug use in the '70s. For the next six years, fearing for his career, he successfully kept his illness a secret from everyone but his wife, casting director Susan Bluestein, their young daughter Alexandra and a few friends.

Davis continued to find work—he won raves as Queeg in a TV version of *The Caine Mutiny Court-Martial*—but ultimately keeping the secret was "very isolating," said Bluestein. "We just couldn't talk to anyone." Davis, 41, had been ready to go public when he entered his final days; in being forthright after his death, Bluestein said she was fulfilling his final wish: "He didn't want to be one more person who said he died of something else."

A young actor, a promising career, a joke gone terribly wrong

JON-ERIK HEXUM

1957–1984

He was a young man on the rise, memorably handsome, building credits and getting noticed in Hollywood. Jon-Erik Hexum, 26, had starred as a time traveler, Phineas Bogg, in the NBC adventure series *Voyagers!* and as the title hunk and object of desire in a Joan Collins made-for-TV movie, *The Making of a Male Model.*

By 1984, he was again starring in a network series, *Cover Up,* about a secret agent posing as a male model. On Oct. 12, during a break in filming, he jokingly put a .44 Magnum revolver near his temple and pulled the trigger. The gun went off with a blast so powerful that the wadding from the blank round fractured his skull. He was rushed to a hospital, but the damage was too great. Six days later he was pronounced brain-dead. Per his family's wishes, many of his organs, including his heart, were donated to help others.

A gun containing blanks kills Bruce Lee's son

BRANDON LEE

1965–1993

The son of martial-arts star Bruce Lee, Brandon Lee grew used to, but didn't always enjoy, the inevitable comparisons. "When you have a built-in comma after your name," he said, "it makes you sensitive."

Especially, no doubt, when you make your living in the same line of work. Filming *The Crow,* about a rock star who comes back from the dead to avenge his own murder, in Wilmington, N.C., the younger Lee had just begun to make a name for himself in action films. Shortly after midnight on March 31, while filming a scene in which his character got shot, he slumped to the floor—but he wasn't acting. Although the gun fired by a fellow actor contained blanks, somehow a metallic fragment ripped through Lee's abdomen and lodged in his spine.

Doctors at a nearby hospital tried for five hours to stop the bleeding. Lee's fiancée, casting assistant Lisa Hutton, 29, arrived shortly before he died. Lee was 28; his father, Bruce, had died of brain edema at 32.

An ordinary day ends in tragedy

HEATHER O'ROURKE

1975–1988

If you ever say the phrase "They're heeeere!" you're quoting child actress Heather O'Rourke, who made the line famous in the spooky 1982 superhit *Poltergeist.* She got her start in almost laughably perfect Hollywood style: *Poltergeist* director Steven Spielberg spotted the Alice-in-Wonderland look-alike in the MGM commissary and signed her for the movie. That $76 million success led to *Poltergeist II* and *III* and helped her family move from a mobile home to much fancier digs in Lakeside, Calif.

Tragedy struck without warning. On a Monday morning Heather, 12, developed flu-like symptoms. Hours later she was rushed to a hospital in septic shock and cardiac arrest. Airlifted to Children's Hospital and Health Center in San Diego, she was operated on for intestinal stenosis, an acute bowel obstruction—a congenital condition neither her mother nor stepfather had suspected. She died on the operating table.

The king of caustic comedy took gleeful aim at sacred cows (and big bugs)

MICHAEL O'DONOGHUE

1940–1994

He appeared in the first sketch of the first episode of *Saturday Night Live,* on Oct 11, 1975, as a language instructor trying to teach English to John Belushi. The phrase Michael O'Donoghue, who wrote the skit, was trying to impart said much about *SNL* in general and about O'Donoghue in particular:
O'Donoghue: "Repeat after me. 'I would like . . .'"
Belushi: "I would like . . ."
O'Donoghue: "To feed your fingertips . . ."
Belushi: "To feed your feen-ger teeps . . ."
O'Donoghue: "To the wolverines."
Belushi: "To duh wol-verines."

Clearly, this was not *Laugh-In* or Carol Burnett or even Sgt. Bilko, and O'Donoghue was not Mr. Rogers (though one of his *SNL* personas, Mr. Mike, whose *Least-Loved Bedtime Stories* frequently ended badly for those involved, was clearly Mr. Rogers's malevolent twin). O'Donoghue's mordant, sometimes shocking humor didn't appeal to everyone, but it did appeal to a vast swath of Baby Boomers who yearned for a little jalapeno, or even some bitter herbs, in the bland TV dinner they'd been served since childhood. His humor helped shape the *National Lampoon* magazine, and he was co-winner of two writing Emmys for his work on *Saturday Night Live* in 1976 and 1977.

He could be droll, and he sometimes—okay, almost always—pushed the limits of good taste. "It's all very easy to laugh at yourself," he once said. "The difficult thing is learning to laugh at others." He remarked that "life is not for everybody" and claimed to be working on something called *The Dairy of Anne Frank,* "in which a plucky little Jewish girl hides from the Nazis in the attic with a herd of cows." "My humor is cruel if you accept *I Love Lucy* as the standard," he once said. "But life in America is pretty violent fare. I just think my humor is accurate reflection of my times. Nobody is painting Botticellis anymore."

O'Donoghue could also, when he wanted, play to a broader audience: He cowrote the screenplay for the Bill Murray Christmas hit *Scrooged* and scored a Top 10 country single with his song "(Single Bars and) Single Women," which became a hit for Dolly Parton.

He died of a brain hemorrhage, at 54, in 1994.

ALEXANDER GODUNOV

1949–1995

A strapping 6'3" dancer, Alexander Godunov stunned Soviet audiences in 1971 when he made his debut in *Swan Lake* at the Bolshoi Ballet. "Everyone was talking about this new dancer with the long blond hair and the Roman face," said Konstantin Kosterev, a friend. "He was a phenomenal success." His defection to the U.S. while touring with the Bolshoi in 1979 almost caused an international crisis.

In New York Godunov joined the American Ballet Theatre, then under the direction of Mikhail Baryshnikov, a friend and rival from their days together as students in Riga. When he was dismissed in 1982—allegedly because there weren't enough good roles for him—Godunov complained that Baryshnikov "threw me away like a potato peel." They never spoke again.

But his love life, and another career, blossomed. Godunov met actress Jacqueline Bisset at a New York party, and the two became inseparable. In 1985 he appeared as an Amish farmer opposite Harrison Ford in *Witness* and three years later as a memorable Euroterrorist in *Die Hard.* Then the work dried out, in part, Bisset suggested, because perfectionism led him to shun challenging roles. "Alexander was his own worst critic," said Bisset, who split with him in 1988, "which sometimes rendered him fearful."

Few knew that in later years Godunov developed a serious drinking problem. He died in May 1995 from the effects of acute alcoholism. "He was a magnificent dancer," said Svetlana Zovorotina, a Bolshoi colleague. "But who knows what went on in his soul?"

Laughter, sadness and drugs: A comic heavyweight who idolized John Belushi meets the same fate

CHRIS FARLEY

1964–1997

Chris Farley, sweat pouring down his face, clutched his chest and yelled, "I'm about to have a heart attack!" It was a joke; partying wildly at the Chicago club Karma, the colossal comic was doling out $50 tips and doing his usual over-the-top comedy bits for fans.

Four days later, on Dec. 18, 1997, Chris's brother John found the 5'8", 296-lb. actor sprawled in the foyer of his 60th-floor apartment, dead, doctors said later, from an accidental drug overdose. In the previous week Farley, who made his name on *Saturday Night Live* and in movies, had freebased cocaine, according to a witness; hit so many clubs that even Chicago Bull's wildman Dennis Rodman, who'd bumped into him, said he was partying "too much"; and hired exotic dancers to entertain him at home. One dancer said she had spent Wednesday, the day before Farley died, watching him consume large quantities of cocaine, heroin and vodka.

"There was a hyperawareness of what was going on with Chris," said former *SNL* castmate Al Franken, but pals—and Farley himself, who had tried numerous stints at rehab—seemed powerless to stop it. Although he made up to $5 million per film, friends say he never felt he fit in. "He always said, 'They come to see the fat boy fall down,'" said a producer who had helped launch his career. "But I don't think he liked being the fat boy." Said his former drug counselor: "Chris thought he needed to be loaded to excess in order to be accepted."

A shy Catholic kid from Wisconsin, Farley, 33, had continued to attend Mass, even on the Sunday before he died. "Lust, gluttony, booze and drugs are most of the things I confess to," he once told a reporter. "I can't help it. I want to be a good Catholic, but I'm a hedonist."

DAVID STRICKLAND

1969–1999

David Strickland could be the life of the party. As the boyish music critic on NBC's *Suddenly Susan,* "[he] held us together because he was so light and fun," said costar Nestor Carbonell. "He was the glue." Recalled a woman who saw him at a Las Vegas club the weekend of his death: "He was jumping around and introducing everyone to his friends, being Mr. Hollywood.... He was happy and joking."

But, as many friends knew, there was also darkness in his life. Around 4 a.m. on March 22, 1999, Strickland, 29, paid $55 for a room at the Oasis, a motel on a sketchy section along the Vegas strip. "He was pretty quiet," said the owner. "He didn't express himself." When Strickland failed to check out by 11 a.m., a desk clerk entered his room and found the actor hanging from a ceiling beam, a bedsheet wrapped around his neck. Six empty beer bottles lay on the floor.

Out of public view, Strickland had long battled drug and alcohol abuse. He was arrested for cocaine possession in 1998 and had been due to appear in court for a progress report on the day he died. "If he had an episode where he fell off the wagon, it would be once every two months," Carbonell later recalled of his friend's struggle. "He'd have a bad episode, and we'd all worry about it for a night or two, and he'd resurface as if nothing had happened. He'd always resurface."

Suddenly Susan star Brooke Shields was heartbroken. "I am devastated," she said, "by the loss of my best friend." Carbonell believed that, ironically, Strickland's recent happiness may have played a role in the tragedy. "The drinking and the drugs were self-medication for him to come down from the high of all the great work and good things," said Carbonell. "He wanted so badly to be able to handle his success."

*A charming Everygirl who made her
name by getting to the church on time*

CHARLOTTE COLEMAN

1968–2001

Barely zipped into a poufy party dress, Charlotte Coleman memorably opened the
1994 movie *Four Weddings and a Funeral* as she scrambled with Hugh Grant to make
it to the church on time. In real life she could be just as quirky. Once, she arrived an
hour late to meet TV producer Roderick Gilchrist and other pals. Her excuse? She
was making a sympathy card for a woman whose mother had just died. "That was
Charlotte," Gilchrist said. "Just when you wanted to shake her, she shook you. She had
a goofball way about her, but that was just surface."

   Her death, sadly, shocked friends as well. The 33-year-old actress died in her London
apartment after suffering a catastrophic asthma attack. "I didn't even realize she *was*
asthmatic," said casting agent John Hubbard. "It took us all by surprise."

*A small actor
dreamed big*

JOSH RYAN EVANS

1982–2002

Making it in Hollywood isn't easy; it's even harder when you're 3′2″. But Josh Ryan Evans never considered his stature an obstacle. "If I was just another blond-haired, brown-eyed actor," he once said, "I'd be left unrecognized."

Evans, 20, caught everyone's attention as Timmy, a spooky living doll on *Passions,* a campy NBC soap that dabbled in the occult. Bizarrely, hours before Evans died of complications from a congenital heart condition, his alter ego was killed off on *Passions.* "The timing is so ghastly, but Josh would have loved that," said Juliet Mills, who played a witch on the popular show. "It's so Hollywood."

Born with achondroplasia, a type of dwarfism, Evans endured several operations as a child. Watching *Star Wars* and other films, he said, "took me away from the hospital and made me think about being an actor."

To the end, said Mills, "he was doing exactly what he had planned to do. He never signed an autograph without writing, 'Dream big.'"

No stranger to tragedy, an actor makes a sad exit

ROBERT PASTORELLI

1954–2004

Robert Pastorelli earned an Emmy nomination for his performance as Eldin, the laconic housepainter to Candice Bergen's newswoman on the sitcom *Murphy Brown*. Even after he left the show in 1994, the New Jersey-bred actor remained a hit with his costars. "Bobby looked great," costar Joe Regalbuto recalled of a 2003 cast reunion. "He had us laughing, like always."

Heartbreak may have been just beneath the surface. In 1999, Pastorelli's girlfriend Charemon Jonovich accidentally shot and killed herself in the couple's home. While raising their 6-year-old daughter Gianna and hunting for work—he'd recently starred as a hit man in the *Get Shorty* sequel *Be Cool*—he apparently began dabbling in drugs. On March 8, 2004, Pastorelli's assistant discovered the actor, 49, dead from what a coroner later determined to be an accidental overdose of heroin. Friends were stunned. "I find it almost impossible to believe," said singer Chuck E. Weiss, a friend. "Bobby had been clean and sober for almost 16 years."

A graceful giant, onscreen and off

MATTHEW McGRORY

1973–2005

Camera tricks made the 7′6″ McGrory (with Ewan McGregor) appear more than 10 ft. tall in 2003's *Big Fish*.

According to the *Guinness Book of World Records,* Matthew McGrory was, at 7′6″, the world's tallest actor and also had the world's largest feet: size $29^{1}/_{2}$. Doctors were never completely sure of the reasons for his extraordinary growth. The Pennsylvania native studied law at Widener University and, not surprisingly, specialized in playing giants onscreen, most notably in the 2003 film *Big Fish*. He died at 32 of natural causes.

Said pal Michael Madsen: "Chris was true blue through and through"

CHRIS PENN

1965–2006

"Acting is the calling of my family," Chris Penn once said. "I don't think I could do anything else."

Indeed: A Penn family Thanksgiving dinner table could include Oscar-winning brother Sean, film composer brother Michael and actress mom Eileen. (Dad Leo, a director, died in 1998.) Chris insisted he didn't measure himself against Sean's success. "I'm my own artist," he said. "Always have been and always will be."

Following a major role in 1984's *Footloose,* he appeared opposite Sean in *At Close Range.* After a late '80s battle with alcohol and cocaine, he said, "[Sean] helped me get my life back on track." So did Quentin Tarantino, who cast Chris as a thug in 1992's *Reservoir Dogs,* which led to parts in *Short Cuts* and *True Romance.*

When Penn, 40, was found dead on Jan. 24, 2006, some suspected illegal drugs might have played a role. But the coroner ruled the actor had succumbed to "nonspecific cardiomyopathy." Prescription drugs found in his system may have added to the problem, but, said a spokesman for the coroner, Penn "just had a bad heart."

MUSICIANS

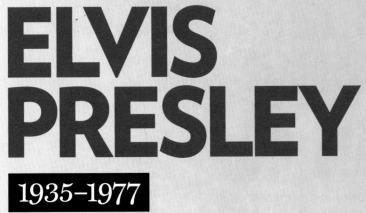

*Farewell
to the King*

ELVIS PRESLEY

1935–1977

Listening to rock and roll, "I can't stand still," said Elvis (right, and in his 1968 TV special, below). "I've tried, and I can't do it."

According to one story, it all started because Elvis was so nervous during his first live performances that his knees shook. Girls started screaming, so he incorporated the twitchiness, augmented by a few gyrations, into his act. The forces of righteousness were duly outraged about this discombobulatingly risqué business: Ed Sullivan, during one Elvis appearance, showed the King only from the waist up and, after a Florida judge ordered him to keep his show clean, Elvis reigned in his wandering pelvis—but, he later joked, nonetheless waggled his little finger to the tune of "Hound Dog" like a mischievous madman. "Momma," he once asked, shortly after embarking on a career that would see him sell more than 500 million records and star in 33 movies, "do you think I'm vulgar on the stage?"

"You're not vulgar," his beloved mother, Gladys, replied. "But you're puttin' too much into your singin'. Keep that up, you won't live to be 30."

In the end, it wasn't the singing, but everything else, that killed him. His wily manager, Col. Tom Parker, who banked a reported 50 percent of Elvis's earnings, milked him like a cash cow, keeping him on a relentless concert schedule (nearly 1,100 shows from 1969 to 1977) and signing him up for quickie movies that often made the rockabilly god look like dancing Velveeta. (Elvis never toured outside the U.S. because, it was later discovered, Parker was an illegal immigrant from Holland, and any trip requiring a passport would have revealed his secret.) Elvis's loyal retainers, aka the Memphis Mafia, spent his money, laughed at his jokes and never said no. Nor, for that matter, did his personal physician, Dr. George Nichopoulos, who was more than willing to treat the singer's ailments, physical or spiritual, with whatever modern pharmacopoeia could provide: *The New York Times* reported that, during the 32-month period before Elvis died in 1977, "Dr. Nick" prescribed 19,000 doses of narcotics, sedatives and stimulants for the King.

Elvis died alone in his bathroom at 42. Traces of at least 10 drugs were found in his blood. Said Linda Thompson, his last long-term girlfriend: "He was like a little child who needed more care than anyone I ever met."

Classic Elvis albums include his first, *Elvis Presley,* and *Blue Hawaii* (below). The King has had more gold and platinum singles than any solo artist in history. His biggest-selling albums? *Elvis' Christmas Album* and *Elvis' Golden Records.*

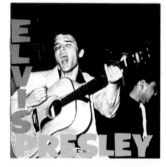

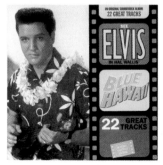

A beautiful bluesman
who did Texas proud

STEVIE RAY VAUGHAN

1954–1990

Blues guitar demigod Stevie Ray Vaughan played, sang, looked and lived the part. Raised in Dallas by blue-collar parents—his dad worked at an asbestos plant; his mom was a secretary at a cement factory—Vaughan dropped out of high school at 17 and began haunting Austin clubs, where his tar-paper voice and bandito hat became as familiar as his physics-defying fretwork. He became a guitarist other guitarists talked about; a videotape sent to Mick Jagger landed him an early New York club date and more exposure. Five albums, including the Grammy-winning *In Step*, followed.

But he was at his best playing live. At the Alpine Valley Music Theater near East Troy, Wis., on Aug. 27, 1990, Vaughan joined fellow bluesmen Eric Clapton, Buddy Guy, Robert Cray and Vaughan's older brother Jimmie for a blistering 20-minute version of "Sweet Home Chicago" to close the show. "It was one of the most incredible sets I ever heard Stevie play," Guy said later. "I had goose bumps."

Afterward Vaughan, 35, boarded a helicopter for the short flight back to Chicago. Moments later all five people on board died in what an aviation official called "a high-energy, high-velocity impact at a shallow angle." Authories, noting that the craft had never gained sufficient altitude to get over surrounding hills, blamed pilot error.

Fans and friends, like Guy, were devastated. "Stevie is the best friend I've ever had," he said, "the best guitarist I've ever heard and the best person anyone will ever want to know."

Mixing spandex and spectacle? He was the champion of the world

FREDDIE MERCURY

1946–1991

Showmanship, thy name was Freddie. The lead singer and a songwriter for the supergroup Queen, Freddie Mercury mixed rock, opera, bombast and bravura to create genre-defying hits like "Bohemian Rhapsody"—which used more than 50 chords—and the now-ubiquitous sports anthem "We Are the Champions." Onstage, spandexed or shirtless, he delighted in the grand gesture and dramatic tableaux; Mercury owned a 20-plus-room mansion in London's Kensington district, but his public persona lived, full tilt and unapologetic, at the corner of rock and rococo.

Before he was Freddie Mercury, he was Farrokh Bulsara, just a kid from Zanzibar (now Tanzania), where his father worked for the British Colonial Office. The family moved to England in the '60s and Mercury joined guitarist Brian May, bassist John Deacon and drummer Robert Taylor to form Queen in the early '70s. From the start, the band seemed to pursue both its music and stage show

Just a boy from Zanzibar: Mercury delighted in the bravura performance (above, in 1986) or his 41st birthday, which reportedly included flamenco dancers, fireworks and a 20-ft.-long cake carried by six waiters.

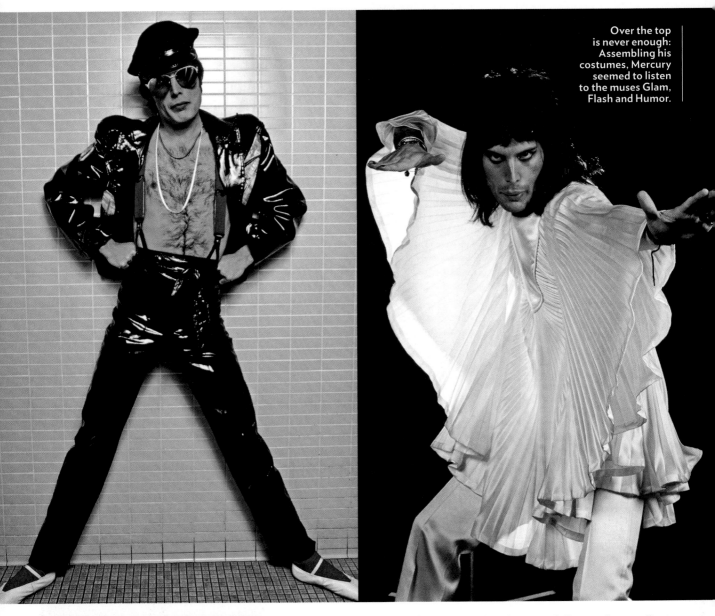

Over the top
is never enough:
Assembling his
costumes, Mercury
seemed to listen
to the muses Glam,
Flash and Humor.

For Queen fans, the mock-operatic
"Bohemian Rhapsody" is the band's signature
song. For sports fans—even, or especially, those
who have no idea who Queen was—that honor
would go the stadium staples "We Will Rock
You" and "We Are the Champions," Queen hits
from the *News of the World* album (above).

with go-for-baroque glee. "Prancing down multilayered catwalks
in a sequinned, skintight jumpsuit and ballet slippers, preening
his way through a myriad of costume changes and singing in his
majestic, slightly frayed tenor voice, Mercury always matched up to
the demands of projecting the group's music and image to the four
corners of the world's biggest auditoriums," wrote a London *Times*
reporter. Or, as another critic put it, "Freddie could be stunningly
tacky, but he'd do it with class and style."

In 1989 Mercury dropped from sight, and rumors began to
circulate that he had AIDS. But the reports of his ill health were
vehemently denied. Then, on Nov. 23, 1991, the 45-year-old singer
released a statement saying he had the disease but "felt it correct
to keep this information private to date in order to protect the
privacy of those around me. However, the time has now come for
my friends and fans around the world to know the truth, and I hope
that everyone will join me, my doctors and all those worldwide
in the fight against this terrible disease." He died the next day, of
bronchial pneumonia.

"Of all the more theatrical performers, Freddie took it further
than the rest," David Bowie told *Rolling Stone*. "And of course, I
always admired a man who wears tights."

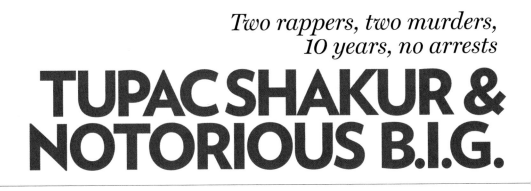

1971–1996

*Two rappers, two murders,
10 years, no arrests*

TUPAC SHAKUR &
NOTORIOUS B.I.G.

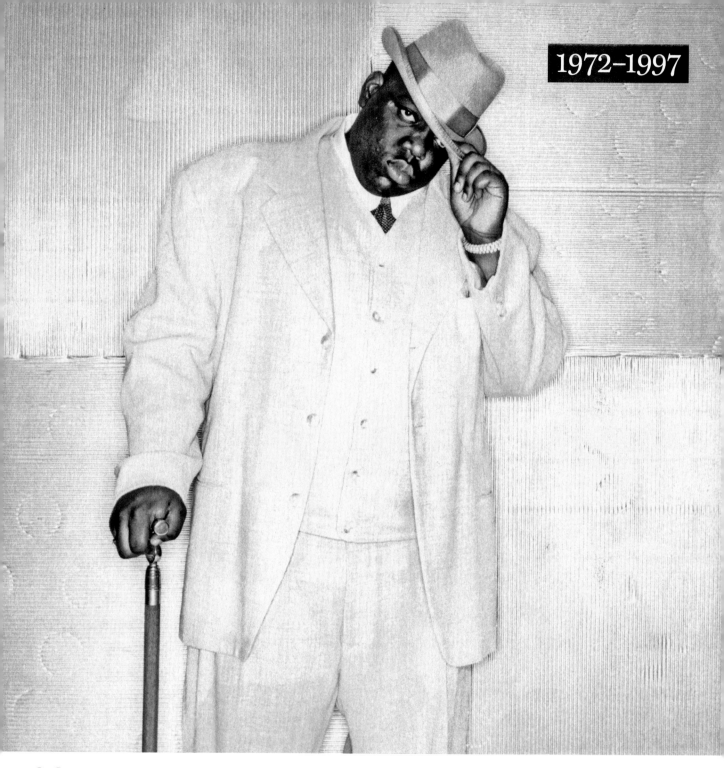

On Sept. 7, 1996, as rapper Tupac Shakur, 25, rode in the passenger seat of a BMW in Las Vegas, a white Cadillac pulled alongside. Two men stepped out and opened fire, hitting Tupac four times. He died six days later.

On March 9, 1997, rapper Christopher Wallace, 24, known to fans as Notorious B.I.G., sat in the passenger seat of a GMC Suburban in Los Angeles. A dark sedan pulled up, and Wallace was showered with fire from a 9-mm. handgun. He was pronounced dead soon after arrival at L.A.'s Cedars-Sinai Medical Center.

More than a decade later, no arrests have been made in the murder of either of the two gangsta rap legends. Some fans and family members say the investigations lacked zeal; police say witnesses have been reluctant to cooperate. Despite rampant rumors, no proof has ever been offered that the two murders are even related.

What is certain: Both men knew they lived risky lives. Shakur, whose raps included "If I Die 2Nite" and "Death Around the Corner," "knew intuitively he wasn't going to live a long time," said a family friend. Three years before his murder, Wallace, whose first, 1.5 million-selling album was called *Ready to Die*, told *Billboard* he favored one particular cut on his new CD: "You're Nobody ('Til Somebody Kills You)."

Stunning family and fans, a charismatic rocker takes his own life

MICHAEL HUTCHENCE

1960–1997

'He was what I call vintage Michael," recalled his father, Kelland, who had dinner near Sydney with his rock-star son on Nov. 21, 1997. "He was just in such great form, laughing, joking, mimicking, like he does."

What happened next stunned everyone who knew Michael Hutchence, 37, the sexy lead singer of the '80s party band INXS: The following morning a maid found him hanging by a leather belt in his suite at the Ritz-Carlton.

The suicide may have resulted from both despair and drugs. Hutchence's blood contained traces of cocaine, Prozac and alcohol; also, that morning, he had reportedly argued viciously with musician Bob Geldof—ex-husband of his lover, Paula Yates (right)—about child custody issues and her ability to travel. "Everyone's just totally baffled," said a friend. "You can only assume that something dreadful happened to him in those hours on Saturday morning."

Sad sequel to a doomed affair

PAULA YATES

1960–2000

A wild woman of the British rock scene, Paula Yates, 40, was married to Live Aid's Bob Geldof when she had a fling with Michael Hutchence. "The first time we went to bed," she said brightly, "he did six things within the first hour I was sure were illegal." Yates and Geldof divorced bitterly; she was linked to alcohol and drugs, and he secured custody of their three daughters. Depressed after Hutchence's death, she said her goal was "to stay alive for another year." On Sept. 17, 2000, she was found dead from an accidental heroin overdose.

For half of Milli Vanilli, a pop song with a tragic ending

ROB PILATUS

1964–1998

One day they were global pop stars with a hit album, *Girl You Know It's True*, a hot video, a tour and a Best New Artist Grammy. The next day, after it was discovered they'd lipsynched their live performances and had sung nary a note on their own album, they were an international punch line.

"We were afraid for two years that this day would come," Rob Pilatus, one half of the duo Milli Vanilli, told the *Los Angeles Times* after the truth became known. "We've cried about it . . . that the secret might come out."

Pilatus returned to Germany, where Milli Vanilli originated, but slid into a drink-and-drugs decline. Despite 10 attempts at rehab, he couldn't shake it. On April 3, 1998, he was found dead in a hotel room near Frankfurt. "He'd been drinking, and his whole body was shivering," said Milli mastermind Frank Farian, who had seen him the day before. "But I [didn't] recognize the danger."

"Milli Vanilli was not a disgrace," said Fabrice Morvan, the duo's other half. "The only disgrace is how Rob died—all alone, destroyed from the rapid rise and then sudden fall." Pilatus was 33.

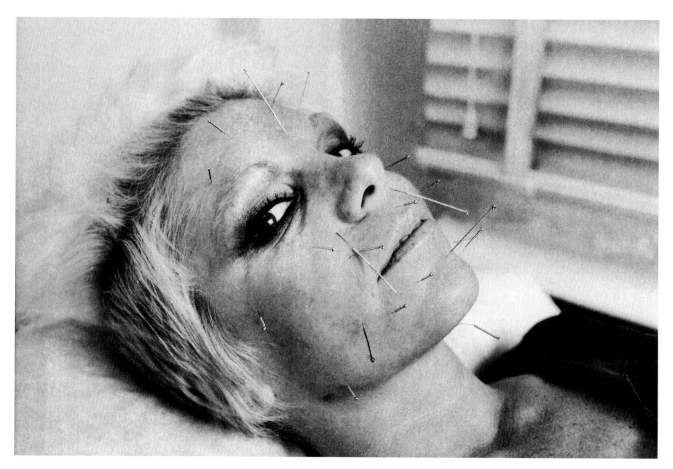

Behind the leather and chain saws, a punk princess with a sweet side

WENDY O. WILLIAMS

1949–1998

Long before Madonna and Courtney Love pushed limits, there was Wendy O. Williams, lead singer of the '80s punk band the Plasmatics. But beneath the platinum Mohawk and taped-over nipples lurked a much tamer soul. "When people met her offstage, they couldn't believe it," said her longtime boyfriend and manager Rod Swenson. "She was very sweet and shy . . . very vulnerable and so sensitive."

Maybe too sensitive. On April 6, 1998, Swenson discovered the 48-year-old singer dead from a self-inflicted gunshot wound. The onetime Queen of Shock Rock, who had attempted suicide twice before, left behind a note that read, "For me, much of the world makes no sense, but my feelings about what I am doing ring loud and clear to an inner ear and a place where there is no self, only calm."

Life was rarely calm for Williams, a wild-child teen who found her calling in 1978, when Swenson created the Plasmatics around her. Known for— among other antics—shredding guitars onstage with a chain saw, she recorded four albums and earned a Grammy nomination before quitting in 1988. Williams later became a wildlife animal rehabilitator but remained unfulfilled. "She tried to hang on," says Swenson. "I was constantly telling her to please not go. Finally, she would say, 'I just need to go. It's better for me to go now.'"

*Beneath the hair
and leather lurked
a punk pioneer with
a sense of humor
and a heart of gold*

JOEY RAMONE

1951–2001

Joey Ramone was loved, and he died the way few rock stars do: not in a plane crash, not in the Chelsea Hotel, but surrounded by his family, who played his favorite bedside song, "In a Little While," a gift from U2's Bono. The tender ballad seemed an apt choice under the circumstances, yet it was also an anomalous one for a punk rocker who once sang, "All the girls are in love with me/ I'm a teenage lobotomy."

Joey Ramone—born Jeffrey Hyman—was a musical rebel who, with three friends from his Queens neighborhood, John Cummings, Douglas (Dee Dee) Colvin and Tommy Erdelyi, formed the Ramones in 1974 and rattled rock music with three-chord sonic blasts and tongue-in-cheek lyrics that riffed on teen sex, suburban malaise and various addictions. With Joey as lead singer on tunes like "I Wanna Be Sedated" and "Now I Wanna Sniff Some Glue," the Ramones "would play 20 short songs in 17 minutes without stopping," recalled Hilly Kristal, owner of New York City's underground rock mecca CBGB.

"No one was calling it punk rock at the time," added Kristal, but the Ramones' 1976 debut album and their British tour that year inspired the rise of even spikier bands, including the Sex Pistols and the Clash. The Ramones disbanded in 1996, after Joey was diagnosed with cancer. Until shortly before he died, at 49, "you wouldn't have known he was sick," said a friend. At over six feet, "he was always a big guy, but his face was so delicate. That's how he looked at the end."

An overloaded plane claims the life of a young singer on the rise

AALIYAH

1979–2001

Twenty-two. That's all: 22. How could so much have happened in such a short time—and how could it have ended so suddenly?

Aaliyah—born Aaliyah Dana Haughton—already had two platinum albums to her credit, two Grammy nominations and had signed to appear in two *Matrix* sequels. Said *Vibe* editor-in-chief Emil Wilbekin: "She had the potential to be the next Whitney, Madonna or Jennifer Lopez."

Aaliyah had spent the morning of Aug. 25 on and around the Bahamian resort island of Abaco, taping a video for her new song "Rock the Boat." That afternoon she and eight others boarded a twin-engine Cessna for the short flight back to Florida. Seconds after takeoff, the plane veered left and crashed. Authorities later determined that the plane was significantly overloaded and that the pilot was not FAA-approved for the aircraft. Friends and family were "devastated," said a cousin. "She was the princess of the family, our baby girl."

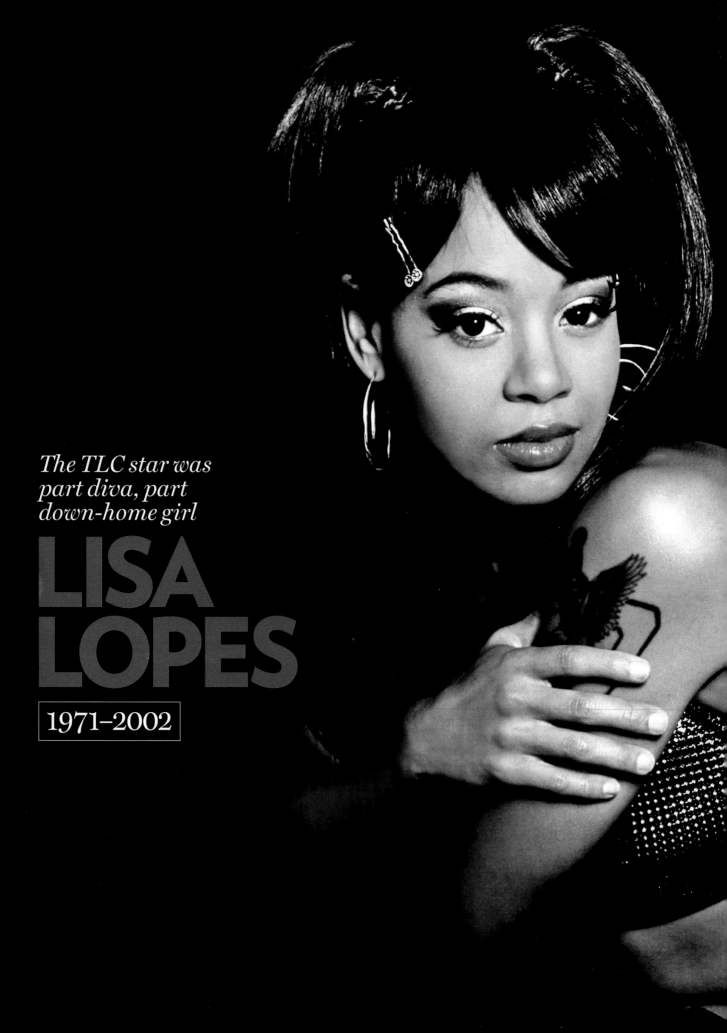

The TLC star was part diva, part down-home girl

LISA LOPES

1971–2002

bush for days." On March 30, 2002, with work on a long-delayed album by her Grammy-winning trio TLC halted by a flare-up of bandmate Tionne "T-Boz" Watkins's sickle-cell anemia, Lopes headed to Central America for a break. She was joined by 12 guests, including members of Egypt–a female quartet from Lopes's native Philadelphia–whom she was mentoring. "She did so much for us," said Egypt's Sophia Gibson, then 19. "She was like an angel."

Their idyll ended horribly on April 25. On the way to a video shoot with Egypt and local children, Lopes, at the wheel of an SUV built for seven but carrying 10, careened off a two-lane highway after passing a pickup truck. Thrown from the van, the singer died from chest and head wounds. Several passengers suffered broken bones. "She was exceeding the speed limit," said the local police chief, who estimated the vehicle was going 85 mph. "There was no indication of drugs or alcohol."

Lopes, 30, who got her nickname from a boyfriend who noticed that her left eye was slightly larger than her right, captured crowds with her flamboyant style and willingness to use TLC's music to tackle social issues. When the band started in 1991, she wore a condom patch over her left eye to promote safe sex. Offstage, there seemed to be two Lisa Lopeses, the local girl who clung close to family, did charity work and still bought her hair extensions at a neighborhood grocery, and the diva-with-a-temper: After a 1994 fight with her boyfriend, pro-football player Andre Rison, Lopes burned down their $1.3 million-dollar Atlanta home.

When the man with the bedroom voice died, a little bit of love went out of the world

LUTHER VANDROSS

1951–2005

Like many of Luther Vandross's close friends, Patti LaBelle never lost hope that the singer famous for his swoon-worthy slow jams would recover from the stroke he suffered in 2003. "I just thought he would be okay," she said. But as time wore on and Vandross's condition failed to significantly improve, "I saw him and I said to myself so many times, 'He'll never sing again, but I'm not gonna let anybody know that,'" she said. "I was keeping hope alive with everybody, I was praying for this miracle."

Sadly, a miraculous recovery eluded Vandross, who died at 54 during physical therapy. He had been dramatically weakened by the stroke, and moments of joking and singing with his loved ones had become sporadic. Still, his death shocked even his inner circle. "There was no turn for the worse," said his business manager, who had visited the singer a week before.

Vandross's only public appearances since the stroke had been videotaped: once with Oprah and once for the Grammy Awards in 2004, to accept his Song of the Year trophy for "Dance with My Father." "He was such a man of dignity," said his friend and frequent songwriting partner Richard Marx, who cowrote "Dance." "The times that I went to see him [after the stroke], my thought was, 'If he really knew what was happening here, he'd be miserable.'" But he did know and was brave.

Gracious, witty and impeccably style-conscious—he rarely took to the stage in anything but a tuxedo and showered his elderly mother, Mary Ida, with designer clothes—Vandross was "just the nicest guy and always sweet and funny as hell," said Kenneth "Babyface" Edmonds. In private he could display a biting wit that was "hilariously caustic," said Marx. "He was one of those guys who, the angrier he got, the more articulate he got. He was razor-sharp."

For his fans, it was the seductive voice—one that "puts you in a space you can't help traveling through," said singer Alicia Keys—that helped Vandross sell more than 30 million albums and win eight Grammys. Said LaBelle: "He had the one and only voice like that in the world. So many people had babies because of Luther Vandross. He made you just want to make love and be happy."

His own life had been marked by sorrow. The youngest of four kids reared in New York City, he lost his father to diabetes when he was 8. Vandross himself battled diabetes, hypertension and obesity—his weight fluctuated from 180 to 320 lbs.—and all three of his siblings died from various health complications. His mother, Mary Ida, "buried all her children," said Nat Adderley Jr., Vandross's longtime musical director. "She outlived all four of them. I'm so sad for her."

ATHLETES

The best pairs skaters in the world, G&G were, above all, a love story

SERGEI GRINKOV

1967–1995

A pair of mismatched children thrown together by the Soviet regime and told to skate for the good of the state, Sergei Grinkov and Ekaterina Gordeeva grew up to become the most celebrated pairs skaters ever—and, while winning numerous world championships and two Olympic gold medals, to fall madly in love. Said former skating champion Dick Button: "God gave them so much—Sergei was the perfect pairs skater, perfect husband, perfect father [to their 3-year-old daughter Daria]. It was as though God had to pull something back."

On Nov. 20, 1995, while training with Gordeeva, 24, in Lake Placid, N.Y., for a *Stars on Ice* tour, Grinkov, 28, complained of dizziness. The couple had just completed a lift, and Gordeeva helped him sit on the ice. Then he fell backward, unconscious.

Katia screamed. Paremedics responded in minutes, and doctors at the Adirondack Medical Center worked on Grinkov for more than an hour, to no avail. "He was dead the moment he hit the ice—he felt no pain," said Dr. Josh Schwartzberg. An autopsy showed Grinkov's heart was enlarged, probably from high blood pressure, and one coronary artery was virtually closed. He had suffered a "silent" heart attack within the previous 24 hours, one that might have caused no pain but may have started a fatal heart rhythm.

Gordeeva's grief "was so powerful, it was heart-wrenching," said Schwartzberg. "She wanted to go in and be with him. I was afraid to leave her alone, but she started speaking in Russian to him in a very gentle, soft and affectionate way. I was very moved by how she caressed and kissed him." Just before she left, she unlaced her husband's skates and gently removed them from his feet. "She was talking to Sergei," a friend, skater Elena Bechke, said later, "telling him, 'Everything will be okay; I will always love you.' I think Katia will be okay too. She will live for Sergei. There will not be another partner for her. They'd won everything together. They were everything together."

Gordeeva continues to perform, but never competed again in pairs. In 2002 she married fellow skater Ilia Kulik, 30.

*The golf world mourns
the loss of a colorful
U.S. Open champion*

PAYNE
STEWART

1957–1999

For a golfer-on-the-go, the day seemed routine: Leave home in Orlando, climb aboard a chartered Learjet and head for Texas a few days before the season-ending Tour Championship to have time to scout out some land on which you might help build a course.

Minutes into the flight, something went wrong: The aircraft did not respond to calls from air traffic controllers. As the plane carrying golfer Payne Stewart, 42, flew on autopilot for more than four hours, his wife, Tracey, frantically tried to contact him by cell phone, the military scambled chase planes and CNN carried much of the drama live. Finally, out of fuel and more than 1,000 miles from its destination, the Learjet plummeted into a pasture near Mina, S.Dak., killing Stewart, his agents Robert Fraley and Van Ardan, pilots Michael Kling and Stephanie Bellegarrigue, and golf-course designer Bruce Borland. Authorities later determined that the plane had lost pressure shortly after takeoff, likely causing all aboard to lose consciousness.

On tour, Stewart, who had won 18 tournaments in 19 years, including three majors, was known as a fierce competitor and a quirky dresser: For years he wore coordinated knickers and tam-o'-shanters. He famously defeated Phil Mickelson for the 1999 U.S. Open by draining a 15-ft. putt on the final hole at Pinehurst, but, asked about his late friend, Mickelson offered up a different cherished memory. "A few years ago we were getting ready to play a practice round, and Payne said, 'I feel so good about my game today that I probably won't even play the last four holes—I'll have you guys closed out by then,'" recalled Mickelson. "When he said that, I took the notebook he kept that told him how he should play each hole and ripped the last four pages out of it. For a second he looked stunned; then he laughed."

Stewart, a father of two, traveled by private jet in part to have more family time, which he craved. "Anytime I called him in Orlando, he was heading to one of the kids' soccer games," said golfer Justin Leonard. "He really got into his family, and that mattered more to him than anything he'd done on the golf course."

*Born to run flat out,
the Intimidator became
NASCAR nobility*

DALE EARNHARDT

1951–2001

He roared through life at his own pace, somewhere around 200 mph. But there was more to Dale Earnhardt's appeal than speed or the way he careened around racetracks with seeming abandon, menacing other drivers with bumper-to-bumper aggressiveness. In many ways he was the modern incarnation of the rural southern male of yore: tough, skeptical, independent, with no back-down in him. "I want to give more than 100 percent every race, and if that's aggressive, then I reckon I am," Earnhardt once said. "It's not a sport for the faint of heart."

His father, Ralph, had been a NASCAR champion. It became clear early that Dale, too, longed to get his hands oily. "I tried ninth grade twice and quit," he said. "Couldn't hang, man, couldn't hang." Dale's decision to work odd jobs while racing on dirt led to some estrangement between father and son. "He was against me dropping out of school to go racing," Dale told the *L.A. Times,* "but he was the biggest influence on my life."

Earnhardt, known as the Intimidator, became the Michael Jordan of his sport, a multimillionaire with an army of ardent fans. "He represented everything you kind of look up to," said one. Said Becky Duckworth, 59—millions of Earnhardt's fans were female—"Besides my husband, Dale Earnhardt is the only man I've ever loved." He acquired all the toys a man could want—Earnhardt owned a jet, a helicopter and a 76-ft. Hatteras, and his mechanics worked in a facility so large they called it the "garage-mahal"—but, as a kid who grew up in the textile mill town of Kannapolis, N.C., he never lost touch with his roots. When North Carolina farmers faced ruin after a flood, Earnhardt, racing writer Ed Hinton recalled, told them, "Just y'all have those damn tractors ready to roll when that seed gets here." "Later," said Hinton, "I learn that the seed he sends them, at his expense, is measured in tons."

Earnhardt, 49, died doing what he loved. On Feb. 18, 2001, seconds from the finish line at the Daytona Speedway, he and Sterling Marlin, battling for third place, bumped cars; Earnhardt spun sideways, was hit by another car and then slammed head-on into a concrete wall. He died instantly from head trauma. Later that year NASCAR began requiring that drivers wear head-and-neck support devices during races.

"I've heard people say we're going too fast," he once said. "Maybe we do, maybe we don't. [But] do you want to race or don't you?"

Tragedy claims the heir to one of NASCAR's greatest legacies

ADAM PETTY

1980–2000

For Adam Petty, 19, speed was a birthright. He was, after all, the fourth-generation heir to stock-car racing's greatest dynasty. "All his dreams and waking moments," said his brother Austin, 18, "he wanted one thing—to race." Like his great-grandfather Lee, his grandfather Richard and his dad, Kyle.

Adam was practicing for the Busch 200 at New Hampshire International Speedway when his Chevrolet Monte Carlo, doing about 130 mph, slammed into the track's outer wall, possibly because his throttle had jammed. He died instantly of severe head trauma.

He and his father were extremely close. "Everywhere you went, they were together," said racer John Andretti. "Every time we were sitting on the starting line, Kyle was right there. Adam would say, 'Dad, I love you. Thanks for giving me all this.'"

Two months later, another wreck

KENNY IRWIN

1969–2000

Just eight weeks after Adam Petty died at New Hampshire International Speedway, driver Kenny Irwin, 30, also crashed fatally—on the same track, at the same turn. In 2002 the track reconfigured the banking in the turns and began adding safety barriers.

*Hooked on flying, a Yankee
pitcher dies doing what he loved*

CORY LIDLE

1972–2006

An aggressive pitcher who had played for
seven major league teams, New York Yankee
Cory Lidle, 34, an amateur pilot, told friends
he planned to fly himself home to California
in the days following his team's season-ending
loss to the Detroit Tigers in 2006. Before
making the trip, however, Lidle and his
instructor took off from a New Jersey
airport for a short spin around
Manhattan. After circling the Statue
of Liberty, the pair headed up
the East River, then attempted a
U-turn in tight quarters—and
crashed head-on into the upper
stories of a high-rise apartment
building. Authorities later
blamed pilot error, although
it could not be determined
whether Lidle or his
instructor had been at
the controls at the
time of the crash.

The death of the Free Willy *whale ended a saga that captured the world's imagination*

KEIKO

1977–2003

Although he died in Norway, Keiko, the killer whale who starred in three *Free Willy* movies, may have suffered from Stockholm syndrome: the tendency of internees, over time, to identify with their captors.

Captured off Iceland in 1979, Keiko became a marine park attraction until the phenomenal success of the *Free Willy* movies sparked an international movement to release him into the wild. More than $20 million was spent training Keiko to survive in the open ocean.

But after his release in Iceland in 2002, Keiko swam 870 miles to a quiet Norwegian fjord, apparently because he liked being around people. He was deluged by visitors until local officials forbade close contact.

Keiko settled in nearby Taknes fjord until he died, from a sudden case of pneumonia, on Dec. 12, 2003. To avoid a media circus, he was buried at night, in a field near the shore, with only a handful of his caretakers in attendance.

CREDITS

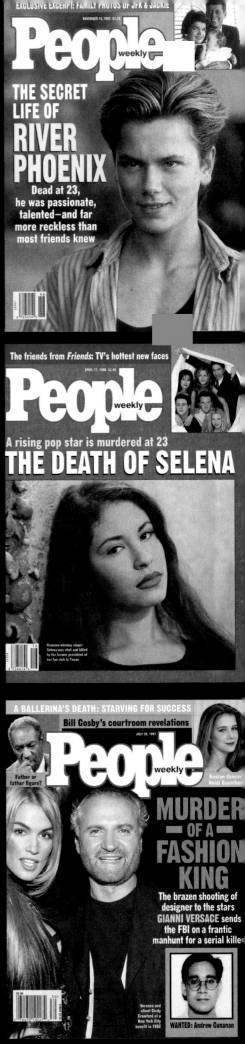

Cover 1 (top-left):

A coma scare for Nirvana's Kurt Cobain

People
weekly

MARCH 21, 1994

ron's new guy

Frank's collapse

Sad death of a funny man

JOHN CANDY

The gifted
comedian
who lived
happily but
too heartily
dies young
at 43

The man of many
faces (from top):
The Great Outdoors,
Who's Harry Crumb?,
Summer Rental and
Spaceballs

Cover 2 (top-middle):

Jackpot in Vegas: Wayne Newton weds

People
weekly

APRIL 25, 1994

NIRVANA'S
KURT
COBAIN
(1967-1994)

His anguished
last days—and
why those who
loved him could
not stop his
tragic death

Cover 3 (top-right):

WHY GENE AND CRAWFORD CALLED IT QUITS

People
weekly

DECEMBER 19, 1994

ONE WOMAN'S COURAGE

ELIZABETH
GLASER
(1947-1994)

She lost her
daughter to AIDS
and was stricken
herself. Then she
found the cause
that sustained
her and gave hope
to thousands
of children

Cover 4 (middle-left):

ALICIA SILVERSTONE: The *Clueless* kid

People
weekly

AUGUST 21, 1995

cole Smith:
now were white

The
Grateful
Dead's
JERRY
GARCIA

The life and times of
rock's happy warrior
(1942-1995)

Cover 5 (middle-middle):

OLYMPICS SPECIAL!
ALL-TIME HEROES: Where are they now?

JULY 15, 1996

People
weekly

Mary Lou Retton, 28, with
her daughter Shayla

MARGAUX
HEMINGWAY
TRAGIC
BEAUTY

She was a supermodel
at 19, then fell hard. Here is
the inside story of her troubled
life—and sad death at 41

Cover 6 (middle-right):

On *Today*'s set as Bryant says bye-bye

JANUARY 20, 1997

People
weekly

Winona Ryder,
free spirit

Heartbreak in Colorado

MURDER
OF A
LITTLE
BEAUTY

The brutal killing
of pageant princess
JonBenét Ramsey, 6,
shocks the nation—
and raises troubling
questions

America's Royal
Miss National

JonBenét winning
a beauty contest,
1996

Cover 7 (bottom-left):

SEPTEMBER 15, 1997

People
weekly

Cover 8 (bottom-middle):

OCTOBER 27, 1997

People
weekly

THE LIFE
& DEATH
OF A
COUNTRY
BOY
JOHN
DENVER
(1943-1997)

Cover 9 (bottom-right):

Cindy Crawford's Surprise Wedding

JUNE 15, 1998

People
weekly

Ginger Spice
takes a hike

Cindy & new hub
Rande Gerber

The Phil Hartman Murder-Suicide

WHAT WENT WRONG

Behind the smiles was a marriage torn by drugs,
threats, and rage that turned deadly

Brynn and Phil Hartman
at an L.A. benefit in 1996

Editor Cutler Durkee
Creative Director Rina Migliaccio
Photography Director Chris Dougherty
Art Director David Jaenisch
Editorial Manager Beth Perry
Designer Patricia Hwang
Photography Editors C. Tiffany Lee,
Judy Watson, Amy Gentle
Reporters Rebecca Dameron, Irina Gonzalez,
Lauren Lazaruk, Hugh McCarten, Vincent R.
Peterson, Brooke Bizzell Stachyra, David Chiu,
Ashton Lattimore
Copy Editor Ben Harte
Production Artists Denise M. Doran,
Cynthia Miele, Daniel J. Neuburger
Scanners Brien Foy, Stephen Pabarue
Imaging Jeff Ingledue, Robert Roszkowski
Special Thanks To Robert Britton,
Céline Wojtala, David Barbee, Jane Bealer,
Sal Covarrúbias, Margery Frohlinger, Charles Nelson,
Ean Sheehy, Jack Styczynski, Patrick Yang

TIME INC. HOME ENTERTAINMENT
Publisher Richard Fraiman
General Manager Steven Sandonato
Executive Director, Marketing Services
Carol Pittard
Director, Retail & Special Sales Tom Mifsud
Director, New Product Development
Peter Harper
Assistant Director, Brand Marketing
Laura Adam
Assistant General Counsel Robin Bierstedt
Book Production Manager Suzanne Janso
Design & Prepress Manager
Anne-Michelle Gallero
Special Thanks To Bozena Bannett, Alexandra
Bliss, Glenn Buonocore, Nina Fleishman, Robert
Marasco, Jonathan Polsky, Brooke Reger, Mary
Sarro-Waite, Ilene Schreider, Adriana Tierno,
Alex Voznesenskiy

ISBN 10: 1-933821-17-5
ISBN 13: 978-1-933821-17-7
Library of Congress Number: 2007906110

MAY 24, 1999

People weekly

PLUS:

Dana Plato
DEATH OF A CHILD STAR

How the cute kid from
Diff'rent Strokes fell
into a life of drugs,
crime and desperation
—and OD'd at 34

Diff'rent Strokes stars Dana Plato, Gary Coleman and Todd Bridges in 1978

AOL Keyword: People

CAMRYN MANHEIM
The Practice star
celebrates her size
in a new book

STAR WARS
Our critic rates
The Phantom Menace

GARTH BROOKS
The winner wore black
at a fashion-savvy
music awards show

AUGUST 2, 1999

People weekly

**John F.
Kennedy Jr.**
1960–1999

CHARMED LIFE, TRAGIC DEATH

**Carolyn Bessette
Kennedy**
1966–1999

AOL Keyword: People

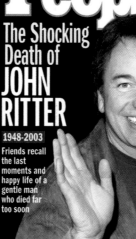

JOHNNY CASH TRIBUTE TO AN AMERICAN LEGEND

SEPTEMBER 29, 2003

People

The Shocking Death of JOHN RITTER

1948-2003

Friends recall
the last
moments and
happy life of a
gentle man
who died far
too soon

BEN & JEN
Will they
reunite?

THE BACHELOR
Bob's back—36
pounds lighter!

TATUM O'NEAL Horrors of a Hollywood ch

OCTOBER 25, 2004

People

Book shocker

HEART OF A HERO

CHRISTOPHER REEVE
1952-2004

· His final days
· Exclusive photos
· The lives he touched

MARC
WE

MARCH 27, 2006

People

AMERICAN IDOL PERSONAL PICTURES

DANA REEVE

Final Days

Only 44, Christopher
Reeve's widow loses her
battle with lung cancer.
Now who will care for
their 13-year-old son Will?

**TERI HATCHER'S
SEX ABUSE
SECRET**

**SHERIDAN &
BOLTON
ENGAGED!**

SEPTEMBER 18, 2006

People

1962-2006

STEVE IRWIN'S Tragic Death

A stingray barb through the heart kills the
beloved Aussie adventurer, who leaves behind
a wife and two children. How did this happen?

**WOW! BODY
AFTER BABY**
How Stars
Slim Down

**MEREDITH
VIEIRA**
Ready for *Today*?

FEBRUARY 26, 2007

People

**Anna Nicole's
MYSTERIOUS DEATH**

BATTLE OVER HER BABY

WHO'S DANNIELYNN'S DAD?
ANNA'S LAST DAYS
THE INHERITANCE FIGHT

Anna Nicole and daughter
Dannielynn on
November 25, 2006

JESSICA
Heat

BEST GR
DRES
Carrie Und

JEN'S BIRTH
PARTY
Vince Shows